D1297673

Exploring Southeast Asia

Also by Milton Osborne

BOOKS

The French Presence in Cochinchina and Cambodia: Rule and Response (1859–1905), 1969; reprinted 1997

Region of Revolt: Focus on Southeast Asia, 1970; revised and expanded edition 1971

Politics and Power in Cambodia: The Sihanouk Years, 1973

River Road to China: The Mekong River Expedition, 1866–1973, 1975; new edition 1996; US edition 1999

Before Kampchea: Preludes to Tragedy, 1979; reprinted 1984

Sihanouk: Prince of Light, Prince of Darkness, 1994; Japanese edition 1996

Southeast Aisa: An Introductory History, 1979; 2nd edition 1983; 3rd edition 1985; Japanese edition 1987; 4th edition 1988; 5th edition 1990; 6th edition 1995; 7th edition 1997; 8th edition 2000; Thai edition 2001

RESEARCH MONOGRAPHS

Singapore and Malaysia, 1964

Strategic Hamlets in South Viet-Nam; A Survey and a Comparison, 1965

Exploring Southeast Asia

A traveller's history of the region

MILTON OSBORNE

CENTRAL ARKANSAS LIBRARY SYSTEM
LITTLE ROCK PUBLIC LIBRARY
100 ROCK STREET
LITTLE ROCK, ARKANSAS 72201

ALLEN&UNWIN

First published in 2002

Copyright © Milton Osborne 2002

All rights reserved. No part of this book may be reproduced or transmitted in any form or by any means, electronic or mechanical, including photocopying, recording or by any information storage and retrieval system, without prior permission in writing from the publisher. The *Australian Copyright Act 1968* (the Act) allows a maximum of one chapter or 10 per cent of this book, whichever is the greater, to be photocopied by any educational institution for its educational purposes provided that the educational institution (or body that administers it) has given a remuneration notice to Copyright Agency Limited (CAL) under the Act.

Illustrations and maps not otherwise acknowledged are the author's own.

Allen & Unwin
83 Alexander Street
Crows Nest NSW 2065
Australia
Phone: (61 2) 8425 0100
Fax: (61 2) 9906 2218
Email: info@allenandunwin.com
Web: www.allenandunwin.com

National Library of Australia
Cataloguing-in-Publication entry:

Osborne, Milton, 1936- .
    Exploring Southeast Asia : a traveller's history of the
    region.

    Bibliography.
    Includes index.
    ISBN 1 86508 812 9.

    1. Asia, Southeastern - History. 2. Asia, Southeastern -
    Politics and government. I. Title.

959

Set in 10/12.4 pt Adobe Caslon by Bookhouse, Sydney
Printed by CMO Image Printing Enterprise, Singapore

10 9 8 7 6 5 4 3 2 1

CENTRAL ARKANSAS LIBRARY SYSTEM
LITTLE ROCK PUBLIC LIBRARY
100 ROCK STREET
LITTLE ROCK, ARKANSAS 72201

Contents

Illustrations

Maps

Diagrams

Graph

In the precious period of cool before sunrise, Borobudur, the great Buddhist stupa in Central Java, looms as a dark mass against the sky. For the moment, its outlines are softened by the early morning mist and the wood smoke drifting from the cooking fires of nearby villages. Very soon, its shape will become clear, sharply defined by the sun's burning rays, for the passage from night to day comes quickly in the lands of Southeast Asia. This is not a region of long, drawn-out twilights and slow changes from a dim light at dawn to the full light of day. And with the sun the vast dimensions of the monument will become apparent. Although at its highest point it rises no more than 35 metres, each of its four sides is 123 metres long, so that a visitor contemplates the terraced mass of a structure conveying a sense of concentrated spiritual power.

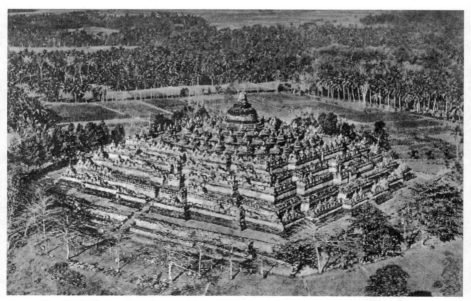

The Borobudur monument in central Java was completed in the ninth century. Massive in size, it was a major site for Buddhist pilgrimages. (PHOTOGRAPH COURTESY OF EDITIONS DIDIER MILLET ARCHIVES)

Introduction

Where the past meets the present

Of all the ancient monuments found in Java, Borobudur is the greatest. It was built at a time when Buddhism was slowly replacing the Hindu beliefs of the Javanese. It is a text in stone. Walking around the five square terraces of the stupa, moving clockwise to mimic the course of the sun, a modern-day visitor gazes at a seemingly endless series of carvings. Here are representations of the Buddhist scriptures and scenes drawn from the life of the Buddha. For countless pilgrims in the past, the act of walking around the stupa was part of a rich spiritual journey and a way to gain merit. To reach the summit of the monument involved walking and climbing no less than five kilometres before ascending the final three circular terraces at the top. There, surrounded by 72 small stupas, each containing a seated statue of the Buddha, it is possible for the first time to appreciate the physical setting of Borobudur in all its splendour.

Built on top of a modest hill, the monument looks out across a lush green landscape towards a

1

ring of towering volcanoes on the northern and eastern horizons. The grandest of these is Mount Merapi, the 'Mountain of Fire', rising 2911 metres, its endlessly smoking summit a constant reminder of its potential for unleashing destructive power, as happened in 1930 when its eruption killed more than a thousand people in a single day. Merapi, the other volcanoes, and the jagged limestone ridges looming away to the south of Borobudur are a reminder of the smallness of man and of the search for spiritual guidance in the face of natural forces beyond human control.

Borobudur was completed in the ninth century CE. ('CE', Common Era, replaces usage of 'AD'.) Imposing as it is, Borobudur is only one of the many monuments dating back more than a thousand years that are located in the richly productive plains of Central Java. Here, too, are the temples of Prambanan, the smaller but no less striking monuments strung out through the Kedu Valley around Borobudur itself, and the less well-known temples of the Dieng Plateau. All testify to the richness of a past civilisation in a region that has been settled for more than two thousand years. Today, the hub of the region is Yogyakarta, a royal city with a well-remembered link to the Indonesian Revolution which won independence from the colonial Dutch in 1949. It is a city with few high-rise buildings and a *kraton*, or palace, built in a traditional architectural style that remains at the centre of its identity. Yet Yogyakarta is also very much part of the modern world. Away from the *kraton*, this is a world of bustling streets and noisy traffic, the site of a major university and a transport hub for the surrounding region.

In contrast, Yogyakarta's 'twin' city, Surakarta (often referred to by its shorter name of Solo), 60 kilometres distant, gives the impression of a location that has only grudgingly surrendered to the demands of the modern world. Like Yogyakarta, Solo is a royal city, housing the palaces of two royal families, Solo's inhabitants claim it maintains a deeper association with traditional arts ranging from music and drama to the production of fine *batik* cloth. With

*Court ceremonies remain important in the
sultanates of central Java. Here, two members
of the Sultan of Solo's court wait for a major
ceremony to begin.*

fewer tourist visitors and a less frenetic street life, Solo clings to
its reputation for refined and timeless elegance.

These two cities and the many monuments lying close to them
are a reminder that the complex past and the often difficult present
are inextricably mixed together in the region that we call Southeast
Asia. It is a world that deserves exploration, rewarding those who
do so with a sense of the region's rich past, its triumphs and its
tragedies.

Legacies of the past

The monuments of Central Java are only one example of the legacy the past has left throughout Southeast Asia in the form of the ruins of ancient cities and abandoned temple complexes. Possibly even better known to outsiders than the monuments of Central Java are the temples of Angkor in Cambodia, and most particularly the greatest of them all, Angkor Wat. Dating from a period between the ninth and fourteenth centuries CE, the temple ruins of Angkor stand as testimony to what was once the greatest land empire in 'classical' Southeast Asia, a period bounded by the seventh and fifteenth centuries. At Pagan, one hundred and fifty kilometres southwest of Mandalay, another great temple complex stands as a reminder of a time when wealth and power was concentrated in this area of Burma (now officially called Myanmar) until the Mongols invaded from China in the thirteenth century. And dating from later periods, there are major monumental remains to be found at Sukhothai, Si Satchinali, and Ayuthia in Thailand.

All of these monuments are linked by common cultural threads to Hinduism and Buddhism, religions that had their origins in India but which came to have their own distinctive character in the countries of Southeast Asia. Their architecture also has links to Indian models, but these were models that were reworked and transformed in their Southeast Asian settings. These local (non-Indian) elements in religion and architecture are two of the more obvious reasons that led scholars in the twentieth century to start talking about Southeast Asia as a region that deserved to be known in its own right and not merely as an extension of other regions. Whatever the cultural inheritance the countries of Southeast Asia received from India, and in Vietnam's case, from China, no-one today would speak of them, as scholars once did, as 'Further India' or 'Little China'.

The Southeast Asian region and its individual countries have only been subjects of study for a relatively short time when

The Thatbinnyu Pahto temple at Pagan. Some 2500 temples and stupas are spread over this great temple site in central Burma, which flourished between the eleventh and thirteenth centuries.

compared to the attention that has been given to the culture and history of Europe, India or China. And where attention has focused on Southeast Asia, there is a tendency to think of the region's history either in terms of the very recent past, or in relation to some of its best-known monumental remains, such as Borobudur, Angkor or Pagan. However understandable it is to think in these terms, to do so is to lose sight of a rich mosaic of events and personalities associated with less well-known periods. And even when the monumental remains scattered throughout the region are recognised for their architectural magnificence, it is frequently the case that too little attention is given to the civilisations that brought them into being.

The temples at Angkor illustrate this fact. There was already a mighty city at Angkor in the eleventh century, with a population of upwards of a million at a time when London was still not England's capital city and had a population of less than forty thousand huddled in a settlement of poor housing and garbage-filled streets. Moreover, with its sophisticated system of water management and the magnificence of its royal court, Angkor was a city whose greatness could impress even the sceptical Chinese visitor who came there in 1267. This man, Chou Ta-kuan (Zhou Daguan in the Pinyin transcription of Chinese) has left us with the only eyewitness account of the Angkorian empire. Or, to take another example, there is no widespread knowledge of the manner in which, seven centuries before Columbus crossed the Atlantic, Indonesian sailors were regularly navigating their fragile vessels from the Straits of Malacca to the ports of southern China, sometimes without an intermediate landfall. These were mighty feats of seamanship linked to an international trade that for a period rivalled the better-known commerce between east and west associated with the Silk Route.

Unity and cohesion in a vast region

To talk of Southeast Asia, as we do today, is to use a term that would have been unfamiliar sixty years ago, except to a few specialists. Before the Second World War, all but one of the eleven countries that today make up Southeast Asia were ruled by colonial powers. Thailand was the exception, but elsewhere Britain ruled over Burma and the regions that now form Malaysia, and Singapore. In addition, Brunei was under British protection. France was the colonial power in Cambodia, the territories that make up modern Laos, and Vietnam. The United States was the colonial power in the Philippines. And in the country that is now by far the largest in Southeast Asia, in terms of population, the Dutch held sway over the Netherlands East Indies, while next-door to the Dutch possession in the western part of Timor, the Portuguese ruled over the tiny colonial enclave of East Timor. So, in the period when colonialism still flourished, it's not surprising that people spoke of 'British Malaya' or 'French Indochina' rather than in the terms familiar to us today.

Beyond the temples with their locally developed architectural character, and the fact that apects of the religions of the region drew on local traditions as well as beliefs that had their origins in India, what were the other reasons that led scholars to argue that there was a Southeast Asian region—a region that had a unity that went beyond the borders colonial rulers had drawn on the map?

Rituals followed in the royal courts of Southeast Asia were, and in some cases still are, an example of shared heritages throughout the region, particularly in mainland states such as Burma, Thailand, Cambodia and Laos, but also extending into the royal courts found in Malaysia and Indonesia. An awareness of the existence of shared languages became one of the most powerful reasons for thinking beyond boundaries imposed by the colonial powers. As linguists studied the mainland of Southeast Asia they became aware that some major languages were not simply confined to a single country. The Tai language, with many differences in dialect, was and is one of the most striking examples of this fact. Tai speakers make up the overwhelming majority of the population of Thailand, but their linguistic cousins are spread over a wide area of the mainland. In Burma, the Shans, a major ethnic minority, are Tai speakers. Tai is spoken in Laos, in the south of China's Yunnan Province, in the northwestern regions of Vietnam, and even in the north of Malaysia in the states of Kelantan and Trengganu (though in this latter case, it is less the case today than was common four or five decades ago).

Another important example of linguistic unity is the broad spread of the Indonesian/Malay language throughout the maritime

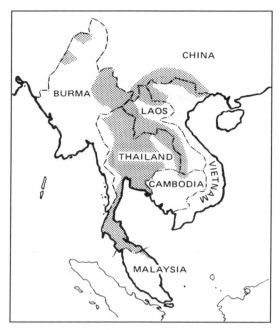

Mainland Southeast Asia: Distribution of Tai-speaking peoples
The Tai language is not only the principal language of the population
of Thailand. It is, in addition, spoken widely by the Shans of Burma,
by the lowland population of Laos, and in the northern parts of
Vietnam, Cambodia and Malaysia. Tai speakers are also to be
found in the extreme south of China.

regions of Southeast Asia. Here, again, there are considerable differences from region to region, from the east coast of peninsular Malaysia to the eastern islands of Indonesia, but variants of the basic language are spoken throughout modern Brunei, Indonesia and Malaysia, in southern Thailand, and in the southern islands of the Philippines. There are even well-established Indonesian/ Malay-speaking communities on the southern coasts of Cambodia and Vietnam.

These are obvious enough examples of linguistic unities that spread across borders that were drawn during colonial times and which with a very few exceptions remain in place today. In some cases, linguistic unities are only apparent to skilled specialists, so that non-specialists find it surprising that Cambodian (a non-tonal language) and Vietnamese (a tonal language) are believed to have a common, if very distant, linguistic ancestor.

The place of the family in society and the status of women were yet other reasons for scholars to start looking at shared characteristics from one country to another. The importance of the nuclear or individual family in much of Southeast Asia contrasts with the importance placed on the extended family in India. And linked to the place of the nuclear as opposed to the extended family was a recognition of the generally important place allotted to women in the peasant society of traditional Southeast Asia. This importance contrasted with the place women occupied in both Chinese and Indian society.

A further step along the path to looking at the region as a whole rather than simply on a country-by-country basis came during the Second World War, when the allied forces fighting Japan established a Southeast Asian Command to distinguish the region from China and India. Then, in the post-war world, historians and political scientists were struck by the range of broad political similarities that could be seen within the countries of Southeast Asia. Here were countries seeking to gain their independence, some through revolution and some by negotiation with the colonial powers. Now there were questions to be asked about why some former colonies avoided revolution, as was the case in Malaysia and the Philippines, while bitter fighting accompanied the revolutions that took place in Indonesia and Vietnam. Southeast Asia came to be seen as a region that was full of interest for the similarities and contrasts found in the region as a whole.

While to speak or write of 'Southeast Asia' has nowadays become commonplace, we often use the term without sufficient thought for just how vast the region is and the great size of some of the national populations within it. These facts become clear when we consider some basic statistics. Of the ten countries that make up the region, five have populations in excess of forty million people. Four—Indonesia, the Philippines, Thailand and Vietnam —have populations over seventy million. What is more, with over 210 million people, Indonesia is the fourth largest country, in terms of population, in the world. In total, Southeast Asia's population represents around 8 per cent of the world's total. With estimates of China's population set at between 20 and 25 per cent of the world's total, the sum of Southeast Asia's population may be seen as sizeable indeed.

Population size of Southeast Asian countries as at 1998 and estimated population in 2025 (figures in millions)

	1998	2025
Brunei	0.3	0.5
Burma (Myanmar)	47	68
Cambodia	11	17
East Timor	0.8	unavailable
Indonesia	205	275
Laos	5	10
Malaysia	22	68
Philippines	73	116
Singapore	3.8	4.3
Thailand	61	71
Vietnam	79	110

Geography, climate and population pressures

The sheer size of the Southeast Asian region, stretching over more than 35 degrees of latitude and nearly 50 degrees of longitude, alerts us to the great variations that exist in the region's physical character. The most obvious differences are those between the countries of mainland Southeast Asia (Burma, Cambodia, Laos, Thailand and Vietnam) and the maritime countries (Brunei, East Timor, Indonesia, Malaysia, the Philippines and Singapore). Throughout history the bulk of the region's population has been concentrated in lowland settlements, along the coasts and by rivers and lakes, but these facts only tell part of the story of geography and human settlement patterns.

Take the example of settlement within a single country, Vietnam. The pattern can vary from the high-density settlement found in the Red River Delta in northern Vietnam to the much less-concentrated settlement found in that country's other major delta region, the Mekong Delta in the south. The settlement patterns in adjacent countries, even along the same river, the Mekong, can be very different, as is the case for Cambodia and Vietnam. With Cambodia's much smaller population (Cambodia's population is about twelve million, Vietnam's over seventy million), there is a very different pattern of agriculture with large areas of arable land left uncultivated. To travel by road from Phnom Penh to Saigon (Ho Chi Minh City) is to see this difference in stark relief. Cambodia's villages appear isolated one from the other, and the countryside is often untilled with only tall sugar palms providing a sense of scale in the flat landscape. Cross the border and there seem to be no areas of land that have been left uncultivated. Villages appear to run together, forming a near-continuous ribbon development along roads and canals. With vast areas of land used to grow rice, there is little place for trees.

There are great contrasts that stem from basic geography, from the difference between hill and valley and between those areas favoured by climate and those where rainfall is infrequent and uncertain. Almost all Southeast Asia lies in the tropical zone, yet this does not mean that tropical abundance is universal. The lives of the hill people who live in the upland regions of Thailand, Burma and Laos, are dictated by their harsh physical environment. They have little in common with those who enjoy the tropical lushness of more favoured regions.

The image of Southeast Asia as an area of lushness, growth and fertility needs considerable qualification. It can be all these things, but it can also be a region where population pressures and the nature of the land mean that life is a continuous battle for survival. Nothing is more misleading than the endless green of ripening crops on the Indonesian island of Java, where an ever-increasing population, now well in excess of 100 million, is jammed into an area little different from that of the United Kingdom, a country with a population of about sixty million and possessing a highly developed industrialised economy. The result for Java is that there are areas of the island where the population has been growing progressively poorer since the nineteenth century, as the number of people supported by the same amount of land grows larger and

A shortage of land suitable for cultivation has often meant that peasant farmers have had to construct terraces in order to grow crops, as seen in this illustration of a rice terrace in Bali.

The summit of Mount Kinabalu in the Malaysian state of Sabah, in northern Borneo. At a height of more than 4000 metres, the mountain is a reminder that Southeast Asia has a very varied topography.

larger. Nevertheless, parts of Java, at least, are favoured by rich soil and predictable rains. By contrast, the shifting cultivators of Laos's uplands must contend with poor soils that mean that they can never hope to achieve more than basic subsistence despite the monsoon rains that pour down each year. Viewing the tiered rice terraces on Bali, another Indonesian island favoured by its soils and its rains, a visitor sees an apparent harmony between man and nature. Too often that same visitor fails to recognise the endless labour that has gone into building and maintaining those terraces. For fertile though the soil may be, the areas available for agriculture in Bali's largely mountainous terrain provide only a limited number of areas where rice may be grown.

The dry zone of Burma, the snow-covered mountains of West Papua and the gaunt, treeless summit of Sabah's Mount Kinabalu are reminders that Southeast Asia's geography is far from uniformly made up of rice fields and palm trees. Neither is there uniformity throughout the Southeast Asian world in terms of where people live. The image of the region consisting largely of peasants living in rural villages is simply no longer true. This was the case a century ago, but the situation is very different today. Singapore, of course, is overwhelmingly urban. It no longer possesses the areas of jungle that once provided a home for man-eating tigers which, according to one resident writing in the 1860s, killed someone on almost a daily basis. It should be noted, though, that 'Stripey', the animal shot dead in the billiards room of Raffles Hotel in 1902, had escaped from a circus rather than the jungle. More surprising to a newcomer to the region is the fact that in both Malaysia and the Philippines more than 40 per cent of the populations live in towns, while even in Indonesia the figure for urban dwellers is over 30 per cent. The contrast lies in the settlement patterns found in both Cambodia and Laos, where 80 per cent of the population still lives outside cities and towns.

Since the Second World War, the fast-growing cities of Southeast Asia have been magnets for rural dwellers who have flocked out of the countryside, where they have seen little hope of change and virtually no prospect of prosperity. Many, perhaps most, have been disappointed with what they have found, but the pull of the cities has remained strong nevertheless. For Thailand's capital, Bangkok, this has meant the growth of the city from a population in 1960 of a million and a half inhabitants to a current population touching eleven million, bringing notoriously enormous traffic jams. Bangkok's story is repeated in other 'primate cities', such as Indonesia's Jakarta. It is not only capital cities that have grown rapidly and dramatically in size. Throughout Southeast Asia, the past five decades have been ones in which urban settlements have been transformed in size; this is true whether considering Chiang Mai in northern Thailand or Davao City on the island of Mindanao in the southern Philippines.

Unity in diversity

'Unity in diversity' is the national motto of Indonesia. Balancing these two concepts against each other will be a persistent theme in the pages that follow, as will an effort to find, in Southeast Asia's past history, events that help us to understand the present. Exploring those past events offers an insight into the life and beliefs of a large and fascinating segment of the world's population. It is a world where religion remains of vital importance. Islam is the dominant religion in Indonesia and Malaysia, while Buddhism predominates in Burma, Cambodia, Laos and Thailand, and is present in a different form in Vietnam. Christianity is the national religion of the Philippines but it has an important role elsewhere

Buddhism is the predominant religion in Burma, Cambodia, Laos and Thailand. The monks seen in this photograph are receiving gifts of food at the beginning of the day.

Islam is a powerful religious force in maritime Southeast Asia. Increasingly its mosques are constructed in a middle eastern architectural style, as seen in this picture of the Sultan Mosque in Singapore.

Christian churches are found throughout Southeast Asia, including Singapore, where this Armenian church is located. Only in the Philippines is Christianity more than a minority religion.

in the region, even in Indonesia. And, in the special case of Bali, a version of Hinduism is embraced by that island's population. There is even a syncretic religion in Vietnam, Cao Daiism, which draws on a range of other religions for its doctrines. It has a hierarchy of cardinals, both male and female, and regards William Shakespeare as a saint.

In terms of cultural achievement, quite apart from contemporary political interest, Southeast Asia warrants more attention than it has received up until now. From the grandeur of the 'classical' years through the transformations that accompanied the arrival and eventual paramountcy of the European powers, from the bitter wars of revolution to the joys and problems of independence—here is a world both waiting and deserving to be better known.

PART I

Southeast Asia
up to the Second
World War

1

Great cities and great empires in the 'Lands of Gold'

Over the past fifty years archaeology, in the absence of written records, has slowly but steadily expanded our knowledge of early Southeast Asia. From archeology we know that there were people living in Southeast Asia who were skilled in casting metals and making pottery as early as 3000 years BCE (Before Common Era). But when it comes to consulting written records it is not until the second and third centuries CE that the first fragmentary sources become available. These exist for the centuries leading up to the classical period in Southeast Asia. This period was remarkable for its significant cultural achievements, and was what might be called Southeast Asia's Golden Age. It was a period in Southeast Asia marked by the emergence of empires that left their mark in the temples of Angkor in Cambodia and monuments such as the Borobudur in central Java, the vast temple complex at Pagan in Burma and the remnants of the temples of Champa, a state that once flourished along the central coast of modern Vietnam. It was also a period in which a very different empire flourished, one that has left only the barest of physical remains. This was the maritime empire of Srivijaya which, with a capital on the Indonesian island of Sumatra, controlled the passage of trade through the Malacca Straits. In discussing this classical period, and in very broad chronological terms, we are talking about the era between the seventh and fifteenth centuries CE.

The inheritance of history

There is one very powerful reason for using the term 'classical' to describe this period in Southeast Asian history. For by doing so we take account of the continuing weight of past history and cultural traditions for the people of contemporary Southeast Asia. Just as the achievements of ancient Greece and Rome are part of the West's collective memory, so an awareness of the greatness of the past is present in the minds of modern Southeast Asians. This is an awareness that exists at various levels, depending most obviously on an individual's education and background. A Javanese peasant may not be able to explain the detailed meaning of the carvings on the temples at Prambanan, but he or she still lives within a cultural environment that has values linking the present with the time when those temples were built.

Cultural memories of the past such as these are not always positive in character. Both Norodom Sihanouk, Cambodia's long-time leader, and Pol Pot, the man who headed the murderous Khmer Rouge regime in the same country, appealed to the memory of the great Angkorian empire as they shaped their twentieth-century policies. They praised Angkor's ability to construct great temples as they tried to transform Cambodia into a state that could stand strong against the threats they saw posed by more powerful neighbours. In Pol Pot's case, his vision that Cambodia could match Angkor's greatness led to terrible tyranny and the death of two million of his compatriots as he presided over an effort to match the great public works of dams and canals built by Angkor's kings.

In the very special case of Vietnam, the one country in Southeast Asia to be deeply influenced by Chinese culture, memories of a different kind have lasted for more than a thousand years. Modern Vietnamese still hold vivid memories of the way in which a great national hero, Ngo Quyen, succeeded in throwing off Chinese political control of their country in 939 CE. In a paradox that is well-known to the Vietnamese themselves, a fierce determination after that date to be independent of China went hand in hand with a readiness to adopt Chinese models of administration, of architecture and of a writing system using Chinese characters. Vietnam's fierce commitment to independence was proudly expressed by a warrior-official, Nguyen Trai, after his countrymen expelled the Chinese after a period of occupation by the Ming dynasty in the fifteenth century. In a poem, ironically written in classical Chinese, Nguyen Trai recalled that:

> Our people long ago established Vietnam as an independent nation
> with its own civilisation.
> We have our own mountains and our own rivers, our own customs
> and traditions,
> And these are different from a foreign country to the north [China].
> We have sometimes been weak and sometimes been strong,
> But we have never lacked for heroes.

The emergence of states and the role of India

To write of Vietnam and how it gained independence from China in the tenth century is to leap far ahead of the time when the first identifiable Southeast Asian states emerge into hazy view in the third and fourth centuries. At that time, Vietnam was an outpost of the Chinese empire with an identity linked to the Red River Delta in the north of modern Vietnam. Even more shadowy were the states in the rest of Southeast Asia. We first know of them from Chinese records and quite recent archeological research. From the sixth century onwards, our knowledge comes increasingly from the translation of inscriptions carved into stone. But before there were political units that can be described as states there were small centres of population that are probably best termed 'settlements'. In attempting to describe these settlements, it's also important to note that there were areas of Southeast Asia in this early period about which we know nothing, or virtually nothing. These were areas that remained outside Western knowledge until a quite late historical date. This is notably so for the eastern islands of modern Indonesia and for all of the Philippines. In the case of the Philippines, before the arrival of Spanish colonisers in the sixteenth century, there are only the briefest records of Chinese trade with that country's northern islands. So our written records start with colonial times and these tell us little about the nature of pre-colonial society.

It is not surprising that the first settlements of which we have any substantial knowledge were established in locations with natural physical advantages. These advantages provided the opportunity for settled populations to grow crops and to catch fish, in contrast to the nomadic life led by hunter-gatherer societies. And since it is clear that these early settlements were linked to an international maritime trade that moved between the east (China) and the west (the Indian sub-continent), they were necessarily located on or near the coast, and usually close to rivers which provided links with their hinterland. The best-known of these settlements, Oc Eo, was established on the coast of what is today southern Vietnam, close to the western edge of the Mekong Delta. (Today, with the steady advance of the coastline as the result of silt brought down the Mekong, Oc Eo's site is now some distance inland.)

The Mekong Delta was a region where human settlement transformed a water-sodden land.

> . . . we must imagine a largely waterlogged world of black mud and mangrove trees, bordered by thick tropical forest where the land rose away from the flooded plain. Drainage canals had only slowly begun to ensure that some areas were protected from the annual floods that came with the rainy season . . . there was so much water that one of the earliest Chinese visitors to the [Mekong] delta wrote of 'sailing through Cambodia'.
>
> Conquering the vast marshy tracts of the Mekong Delta was a necessity for the rise of the earliest settlements in areas that were to become part, many centuries later, of Cambodia and Vietnam. This necessity is captured in one of the Cambodian national birth legends, which tells of the arrival of a prince from India, named Kambu, who married the daughter of the Naga King, or Serpent Spirit of the Waters, who ruled over the land that was to become Cambodia. Approving of the union between Kambu and his daughter, Soma, the Naga King used his magic powers to drink the waters covering the land where the couple were to live. There could be few more graphic affirmations of the importance of the slow but essential battle waged by the delta's earliest inhabitants to transform the environment.

(MILTON OSBORNE, *THE MEKONG: TURBULENT PAST, UNCERTAIN FUTURE*, 2000)

If we try to imagine what Oc Eo, and dozens of other small settlements along the coastline of modern Thailand and Malaysia, might have looked like, we should picture them as pockets of occupation in cleared land that had once been part of a vast forest or a swampy coastal marsh. In Oc Eo's case, aerial photographs have revealed traces of major canals that were built to aid both transport and drainage. And objects found by archeologists at Oc Eo make clear that this settlement had trade links which extended as far afield as the Roman Mediterranean to the west, and China to the east. But it is only with later Chinese written records, and then with inscriptions engraved on stone, that we begin to gain a picture of the type of states that slowly came into being in Southeast Asia. It is with this later evidence that we encounter the important influence that Indian culture had in the region.

For decades there has been a debate as to how Indian culture came to play its part in the early and classical period of Southeast Asian history and about the degree of its importance. There is still no absolute certainty about these issues, but there is now a generally shared set of conclusions. It is generally agreed there was never any major migration of people from India to Southeast Asia. Instead, a limited number of people travelled to Southeast Asia from India. Some of these were Brahmins (Hindu priests), some were Buddhist monks, and some were traders searching for routes to replace the overland routes to China through Central Asia. In part, the traders travelled to the east from India because of a decision made by the Roman Emperor Vespasian who, in the first century, had banned the export of gold to India. Searching for a new source of gold, they looked to Southeast Asia, which became known as 'the lands' or 'islands of gold'. Once the Indian priests and monks reached the small states that were beginning to emerge in Southeast Asia, they found that their religions, Hinduism and Buddhism, proved attractive to the local rulers and their subjects. There is a contrary point of view, which places greater emphasis on Southeast Asians travelling to India. There, according to this view, they embraced Indian religions and culture before returning to their homelands.

A prime reason why Indian cultural ideas gained a foothold in Southeast Asia was that they fitted easily with the religions and beliefs already existing there. Take the example of the importance attached in the Hindu religion to the *lingam*, a representation in stone of the Hindu god Shiva's phallus and so symbolising both divine and earthly generative powers. Indian veneration of the *lingam* is believed to have fitted well with a similar veneration in Southeast Asia of erect stones as fertility symbols. What is more, there was a highly practical aspect to the process being described, for the Indian priests, and perhaps some who simply claimed to be priests, were custodians of knowledge that was very useful to the Southeast Asian rulers they now met. The knowledge of Indian culture that was brought to Southeast Asia did not just relate to religious concepts. In a way similar to the role of the learned clergy of medieval Europe, Hindu priests and Buddhist monks were also men with a knowledge of astronomy and astrology, of architecture and of statecraft. Men such as these could advise a ruler on how to deal with his neighbours, on how to construct a temple and when to expect a major astronomical event, with all the spiritual symbolism that was attached to great natural events such as eclipses of the sun.

Yet whatever the importance of imported Indian knowledge and its convergence with existing beliefs, there were some vital aspects of Southeast Asian life that appear not to have required any foreign input. Probably most important were the agricultural techniques involved in wet-rice cultivation. This fundamental contribution to establishing settled communities was indigenous to the Southeast Asian region, wherever else it developed.

The rich horde of inscriptions associated with Cambodia provide a detailed account of the role played by Brahmin priests in the Angkorian empire. But this was not a simple transplantation of India into Southeast Asia. Some priests continued to come from India, but by the time of the classical period, most of those performing priestly duties were local men. And while Indian culture exercised an important influence over parts of Southeast Asia, in doing so it was transformed by local circumstances. There is, for instance, much overlapping of religious symbolism between the temples of Southeast Asia and those of India, but they are not the same. The great temples at Angkor, or Pagan, or Prambanan, are visibly different from the equally famous Indian temples at Orissa. The Southeast Asian temples are marked by local genius, however much they drew on Indian models. The central towers that represent the homes of the gods are shaped differently, and the Buddhist stupas found throughout mainland Southeast Asia have their own distinctive shape. Difference is readily observable

The Hindu temples of Bali are strikingly distinctive in their architectural character. The temples shown here are at Pura Taman Ayun, near Mengwi, Bali.

in the sculpture and other plastic arts found in Southeast Asia, so that when viewed together there is no difficulty in separating one from the other. Moreover, whatever the importance of Indian influences, some of the most fundamental aspects of Indian culture were never transferred to Southeast Asia. Notably, the rigid Hindu caste system never took root in Southeast Asia, despite the use of caste terms that can be found in early inscriptions and the use of caste terms in modern Bali.

The rise and fall of two great empires

In any discussion of the classical period of early Southeast Asian history, two very different examples of early empires have attracted particular attention—the land-based empire of Angkor, located in modern Cambodia, and the maritime empire of Srivijaya, with its principal base on the Indonesian island of Sumatra. Concentrating on these two empires does not diminish the importance of the other states that grew to power in central Java, around the great Burmese temple complex at Pagan, or in Champa. Neither does it mean the particular case of Vietnam can be neglected. It is simply that Angkor and Srivijaya are the most striking, and, at the same time, very different examples of the kinds of states that existed in the early or classical period. Moreover, in contrast to some other states that existed in classical times, the empires associated with Angkor and Srivijaya were important over a long historical period.

The glory of Angkor

Angkor rose to a dominating position over much of mainland Southeast Asia as a result of a remarkable combination of human genius, religious belief and geographical location. Yet many of the details explaining Angkor's rise to glory are either unknown or a cause for the familiar disputes that are associated with efforts to breathe life into a historical period where the evidence is often limited.

We do know, for this is quite clear from the inscriptions that form such an important part of our knowledge of Angkorian Cambodia, that in 802 CE, a dynamic ruler, known to us as Jayavarman II, took the Angkorian throne. In doing so, he brought unity to what appears to have been a series of small states located in the territory of modern Cambodia. Instead of linking himself with these small states that existed in the seventh and eighth centuries, Jayavarman established a new capital in the region that was to be the centre of Cambodian power for the following six centuries. Not all of Jayavarman's successors matched his talents, but the evidence is clear that enough of them did for them to be able to build the most remarkable collection of great temples to be found anywhere in Southeast Asia. And these temple were not just built in the region close to the modern provincial town of Siemreap but extended throughout the territory of what is now modern Cambodia, and also into modern Thailand and Laos. To build these temples required the mobilisation of enormous manpower. Angkor Wat, the largest religious monument ever to be built anywhere in the world, was completed in the remarkably short time of about thirty-five years during the reign of Surya-varman II (1113–50). This was achieved in a city that had a population that is estimated to have been around one million.

The size of Angkor's population gives a clue to the state's character. Angkorian Cambodia's wealth lay in people and agri-cultural capacity. Certainly, wealth came into the city in the form of captured booty and prisoners of war who were put to work as slaves. But in the broadest sense, Angkorian Cambodia did not depend on trade for its existence. The temples built by its rulers, and in some cases by their great officials, were dedicated to the religions of the state, sometimes Hindu, sometimes Buddhist, and sometimes both together. The wealth needed to build and maintain them and to feed and clothe the priestly communities associated with them came from productive rice fields close to the temples.

It was once thought that the massive reservoirs built near the temple complex, and the intricate system of moats and canals which functioned during the city's heyday, were of practical importance for agricultural irrigation and served as symbolic representations of the 'seas' of the Hindu universe. This view has been called into question as experts have argued that, vast though they were, the reservoirs did not hold sufficient water to supply the needs of large-scale agriculture. The reservoirs, it is now suggested, may well have been used for domestic purposes, such as providing drinking water. The moats and canals did, indeed, have a symbolic character as 'seas' surrounding temples that were themselves earthly versions of Mount Meru, the centre of the Hindu and Buddhist universe and the abode of the gods. But it seems much more likely that irrigation for the three rice crops that were grown each year at Angkor involved the skilful harnessing of the rise and fall in the level of Cambodia's Great Lake, located near the temples. Whatever was the case, Angkor's rulers were able to exercise control over a population that could simultaneously grow the crops to sustain itself *and* build great temples. They did this, what is more, while engaging in wars against internal rebellions and the threats posed by another powerful kingdom,

Of all the monuments that have survived from the classical period of Southeast Asia, those of the Angkor complex in northern Cambodia are among the grandest. Built between the tenth and fourteenth centuries, the temples are scattered over an area of some 200 square miles. the most notable, and probably the largest religious monument ever built, is Angkor Wat, shown here from its western approach. (PHOTOGRAPH BY OLIVER HOWES)

Champa, that rose to power on the coast of what is today central Vietnam.

Because it is once again possible to visit Angkor, it is worthwhile citing statistics that might otherwise risk seeming meaningless, or of little value. Angkor Wat, built in the first half of the twelfth century, measures 202.9 metres (669 feet) by 220.2 metres (726 feet) at its base. The exquisitely carved low reliefs along its principal galleries stretch for nearly 700 metres (2296 feet). There are no fewer than 1750 beautiful carvings of *apsaras* or celestial nymphs that decorate Angkor Wat's walls, with no one *apsara* depicted in exactly the same manner. And it is not only size that impresses in relation to Angkor Wat. Research continues to unlock the temple's secrets. Some of the latest findings suggest that part of the explanation for the extraordinary precision of its construction lies in the fact that it played a part in the astronomical observations of the priests who officiated within its walls.

Angkor Thom, the city Jayavarman VII built during his turbulent reign from 1181 to 1219, was enclosed within a mighty wall 3 kilometres (1.875 miles) square, rising to a height of 8 metres (26 feet). Yet this vast construction, and the state temple within it, the Bayon, were only a part of Jayavarman VII's remarkable building program. Jayavarman VII is a fascinating figure for historians of Angkor. Not only did he build more temples than any other ruler, he left behind inscriptions that hint at his personal feelings. Of these, the most famous is that linked to the 102 'hospitals' he founded throughout his kingdom. In this inscription, he noted:

People's sickness of body became for him a sickness of the soul, so much more afflicting; for it is the suffering of their subjects that makes kings suffer, and not their own suffering.

(CLAUDE JACQUES, *ANGKOR*, 1999)

While Jayavarman VII ruled, there was a frenzy of construction throughout the Angkorian empire as temples, hospitals and strategic roads were built. Thought of in terms of human activity,

In a low-relief carving on the Bayon temple at Angkor, generals mounted on elephants are shown leading their troops into battle. This temple was built by Jayavarman VII.

the picture that emerges is of the enormous and effective use of human resources. Even if much of this labour was undertaken by workers who had little if any choice but to strain and put vast blocks of stone in place under threat of the overseer's lash, it is hard to believe this was the case with the artists and artisans who were responsible for the mass of carvings decorating Angkor's temples. It seems impossible that their work was the product of forced labour. We do not know their numbers, but there must have been tens of thousands of these skilled workers. In some cases we do know how many individuals were required to service temples built during Jayavarman VII's reign. The inscriptions tell us that Preah Khan, a temple-university, required the support of 13 500 villages with a population of 97 840 people, who supplied no less than six tons of rice each day for the personnel associated with the temple. For Ta Prohm, another temple nearby, there was a staff of no less than 12 640 supported by 79 365 people in the

The mighty Ta Prohm temple at Angkor has been left with the trees of the invading forest still growing through its ruins.

villages linked to this foundation. The precision of these figures is striking, and it may be that there is an element of exaggeration, but probably very little.

It is possible to make such a surprisingly confident judgment because we have an eyewitness account of Angkor dating from the late thirteenth century which makes clear just how large were the human resources available to the Cambodian ruler. This, the only eyewitness account of the great city, gains added importance because its author was an openly sceptical Chinese envoy named Chou Ta-kuan (Zhou Daguan in Pinyin). He came to the city in 1286 and stayed there for nearly a year. He compiled a detailed record of what he saw, as well as providing some dubious anecdotes about matters that were hidden from him, in a report to the Chinese court under the title *The Customs of Cambodia*.

In a classic display of Chinese disdain, Chou comments on Cambodian women who, he observes, 'make water standing up—

an utterly ridiculous procedure'. But after offering a wide-eyed account of priests deflowering virgins, he admits he is only recounting hearsay. Yet for all his Chinese sense of superiority towards a people he regarded as 'barbarians', Chou provides what is clearly accurate detail on issues ranging from agriculture and the presence of slaves to the clothing worn by the population. And, importantly, he describes some of the major temples in a manner that allows us to sense their greatness while the Cambodian court still lived at Angkor. When Chou Ta-kuan saw them, the temple towers of these great stone monuments shone with gilding or gleaming brass. Summing up his reaction to the city's architectural wonders, he notes that these are 'monuments which have caused merchants from overseas to speak so often of "Cambodia the rich and noble".'

Of all Chou Ta-kuan's fascinating descriptions, none is more striking or revealing of the sense of majesty present in the Angkorian court than his account of the ruler going forth in procession. Chou writes of the Angkorian ruler being preceded by hundreds of young girls carrying candles and of others carrying lances and spears. He describes ministers and princes mounted on elephants, goat carts and horse carts decorated in gold, and the ruler's wives and concubines riding in palanquins, in carts, on horses and on elephants. Then, in the middle of the mighty procession, he describes the king himself 'standing erect on an elephant and holding in his hand the sacred sword. This elephant, his tusks sheathed in gold, was accompanied by bearers of twenty white parasols with golden shafts.' The sceptical Chinese envoy was impressed despite himself, so much so that he is forced to end his description with the admission that 'it is plain to see that these people, though barbarians, know what is due to a prince'.

Yet a little more than a century later, in the first half of the fifteenth century, the Cambodian court abandoned Angkor. The empire of which Angkor had been the centre had survived over the centuries so long as the reigning king was not challenged by the lesser rulers—men whom we might call princes, or governors.

They were the men who controlled the outer regions of the empire but swore allegiance to their sovereign at the centre of the state. When some of these lesser rulers no longer accepted this situation and chose to fight for their independence, they shattered a long-existing political arrangement. In addition, they threatened and eventually damaged the agricultural system on which Angkor's very existence depended. The decision of the Cambodian king to leave Angkor was of the deepest importance for mainland Southeast Asia, yet it was an event quite unknown in distant Europe. The Thais, a formerly subject people who had once formed part of the Cambodian king's army, brought Angkor down and their history from that time onwards was marked by a slow but sure progress towards the achievement of control over the territories that comprise modern Thailand.

The departure of the Cambodian ruler from Angkor and the emergence of newly powerful states in the central Thai plain, notably at Sukhothai and Ayuthia, was part of a broader pattern that saw the reordering of mainland Southeast Asia's political map. Cambodia's weakness ultimately provided the independent Vietnamese state, free of Chinese control, with opportunities for territorial expansion into what had once been part of the Angkorian empire in the south of modern Vietnam. But in the fifteenth century, this expansion was still far in the future. More immediately, as Vietnam maintained its independence from China, it was steadily dismembering the state of Champa, which had once been able to challenge Angkor's power.

To the west again of Thailand, in what is today modern Burma (Myanmar), a great city had been built between the eleventh and thirteenth centuries at Pagan, an inland site on the Irrawaddy River. Deeply influenced by Buddhism, the rulers of Pagan constructed hundreds of temples, many of which remain to be admired today. Yet while there were periods when Pagan was a powerful state, it ultimately fell following a Mongol invasion in 1287, when these warriors from the Central Asian steppes ruled

China. In the subsequent centuries, no Burmese state ever exercised power to match that which had existed at Pagan.

The maritime empire of Srivijaya

Angkor was the most powerful of Southeast Asia's land-based states for which trade was a secondary concern. In contrast, Srivijaya rose to greatness as a maritime trading power controlling the Straits of Malacca, becoming the most successful such power in this early phase of Southeast Asia's history. With its trading character, Srivijaya differed, too, from the land-based kingdoms that had emerged in central Java and which were responsible for the monuments discussed at the beginning of the Introduction—Borobudur and the temples of Prambanan. We know tantalisingly little about these states, so that it is something of a surprise to realise that it is possible to write with some degree of confidence about Srivijaya, even though its very existence was unknown in the West until the early part of the twentieth century. Research in Chinese records and obscure inscriptions yielded up information that enabled a French historian to identify this important early Southeast Asian state.

Srivijaya's rise to power depended on trade and on China's sponsorship. From the earliest records we have of Southeast Asian history there was, as excavations at Oc Eo have shown, an international trade that extended from China to the Indian sub-continent and beyond, into the Mediterranean world. Precious Western goods, including forest products believed to have medicinal qualities, were exchanged in China for silks, porcelains and lacquers. By the seventh century, control of much of this trade passing backwards and forwards between the Indonesian islands was in the hands of Malays whose chief centre of power was on or close to the coast of southeastern Sumatra. How this came about is uncertain, as is the explanation of how the sailors who manned the ships that carried the trade goods navigated the route to China with few, if any, landfalls along the way. What we do know is that China's role in this trading pattern was vital.

Whether strong or weak, the successive rulers of China regarded their kingdom as the central world state, the 'Middle Kingdom' in their own words. The states of Southeast Asia were, in Chinese eyes, inhabited by people who, through not being Chinese, were in various ways inferior. They were, as Chou Ta-kuan described the Cambodians at Angkor, 'barbarians' who lacked a proper understanding of a culture that had developed in China for over two thousand years. Vietnam was an irritating, partial exception to this judgment. For not only had China administered Vietnam until 939, even after that date the men who ruled an independent Vietnam did so in a manner that drew heavily on Chinese models. This paradoxical situation has led to Vietnam's relations with China being difficult over the centuries. Yet despite shared cultural values, China expected Vietnam, just as it expected the other states of Southeast Asia which had been influenced by Indian culture, to acknowledge its central world role. In the terms that have become widely accepted, China expected the states of Southeast Asia to be its tributaries.

The concept of tributary relationships is not always easy to understand. It did not mean that an individual Southeast Asian state was ruled by China and formed part of some ill-defined Chinese empire. Rather, the tributary relationship was one that involved a good deal of give and take. As a Chinese tributary, a Southeast Asian state was expected to give due consideration to Chinese interests—the fact that Vietnam repeatedly failed to do so was a cause of constant friction. But provided a tributary state showed the correct degree of respect, then the expectation was that China would protect its tributary's interests. Because these tributary relationships seem foreign to modern observers, it is worth emphasising that apart from Vietnam, no other state in Southeast Asia was ever ruled by China. Moreover, only one dynasty, the foreign Mongol or Yuan dynasty that ruled China from 1280 to 1368, ever sought to impose its authority over the states of Southeast Asia by force.

China's role was vital for the emergence of Srivijaya as a major maritime power, for being accepted as a tributary state was linked to the right to trade with China—Angkor, too, was a tributary, but its relationship with China was not linked to trade. Once China had granted tributary status to Srivijaya, the maritime states that were its rivals were at a severe disadvantage and Srivijaya's own capabilities brought it to the forefront of Southeast Asian maritime power. Strategically placed on the Malacca Straits, Srivijaya was able to control all significant trade on the seas in the western section of the Indonesian Archipelago, and between that region of the Archipelago and southern China. Srivijaya's capital was probably located in more than one place over its long existence,

A low-relief carving of a ship at the Borobudur monument in Java. The ships used by the sailors of Srivijaya would have been similar to this craft. (COURTESY OF EDITIONS DIDIER MILLET ARCHIVES/PHOTOGRAPHER TARA SOSROWARDOYO)

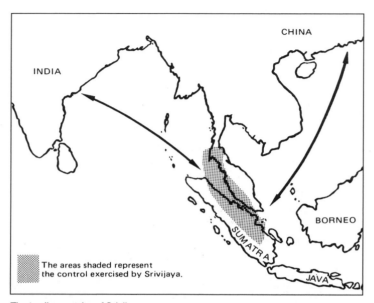

The trading empire of Srivijaya
Scholars argue over the exact location of Srivijaya, the great trading empire that dominated maritime trade through Southeast Asia and between India and China during the seventh to thirteenth centuries. Srivijaya probably had a number of capitals, with the most important in southern Sumatra, adjoining modern Palembang. As indicated in this map, Srivijaya maintained its power by controlling the ports and waters of the Malacca Straits. The shaded areas represent the control exercised by Srivijaya.

but there is convincing evidence that one of these locations—and possibly where the capital was based for the longest period—was near the modern Sumatran city of Palembang. Probably the capital was only slightly more important than the other port cities and trading settlements that made up this maritime trading empire. For any state or settlement that challenged the Srivijayan trade monopoly, we can suppose that retribution was swift. But we can also suppose that Srivijaya exercised a light hand over its outposts, always so long as the basic trading arrangements were not infringed.

It was an empire that was adapted to its environment, with the sea as its open frontier to make up for the lack of a readily cultivable hinterland along the swampy southeastern coast of Sumatra and the western coast of modern peninsular Malaysia. For upwards of seven centuries, Srivijaya maintained its role as an entrepôt, foreshadowing the later importance of Malacca and even, eventually, Singapore. It was the first to show how vital control of the seas could be. Few of the Portuguese, Dutch or British traders and strategists who fought and manoeuvred to gain dominance over the Southeast Asian sea trading routes from the sixteenth century onwards realised that they were successors of earlier maritime empires. None knew that Srivijaya had existed, but in their search for the control of trade and the establishment of an entrepôt, they were following a very old pattern.

Yet just as Srivijaya, like Angkor, was adapted to its environment, so too was it unable to survive when that environment changed radically. Change came in the thirteenth century when the Chinese themselves decided to sail their own trading vessels into the southern seas. Adding to this challenge was the emergence of new, powerful land-based states in Java which cherished imperial ambitions of their own. With Srivijaya already weakened by the arrival of the Chinese traders and threatened by the growing power of the Thai kingdoms in the Chao Phraya (Menam) valley, the Javanese state of Singasari struck a deadly blow. These various challenges brought an end to Srivijaya's long history of dominance over the east–west trade.

The people of the early empires

Anyone writing about the classical period of Southeast Asian history faces the difficulty, indeed near-impossibility, of offering anything like a rounded picture of the ordinary people who lived in Angkor or Srivijaya, or any of the other states that have been mentioned. We are dealing with courts and kings rather than the artisans who carved the bas-reliefs on the walls of the temples of Angkor and the seamen of Srivijaya who sailed their fragile vessels across the empty stretches of the South China Sea. In some cases we know of them in terms of numbers, but never in terms of personalities. And the same comment is largely true even when we deal with the kings of this early period. What are we to make of an inscription praising a seventh century Cambodian king on the grounds that the women of his court felt it would be worth rape by the enemy to enjoy the reward of his smile? Was this simply a routine symbolic compliment, however offensive it may seem today? Or was it an accurate description of how his courtiers regarded a man who was a forerunner of later believers in male dominance? And how should we judge the inscriptions from Jayavarman VII's reign which claimed that he felt his subjects' pain

The bas-relief decorating the late thirteenth century Bayon temple at Angkor are remarkable for combining narrative depictions of recent historical events with scenes from everyday life. In this illustration the central part of the carving shows Cham war canoes on their way to attack Angkor while below are Cambodians watching a cock fight, playing dice and blowing on a flute.

more than his own, or described his grief at the death of his queen? Were these genuine accounts of his feelings? We simply cannot give any certain answer to these questions.

To return to the problem of breathing life into the ordinary people of classical Southeast Asia, the best we can do is to work from the few glimpses of everyday life that are available to us. One source of these glimpses are the bas-reliefs found on the walls of the Bayon temple at Angkor, the most important of Jayavarman VII's many foundations dating from the late thirteenth century. Below the bas-reliefs that record great royal events, such as battles and processions, are scenes of everyday life, of women in childbirth, of men gambling, watching cockfights and ploughing fields. They are fascinating, but tell us only a little of the detail of daily life at the village level. From Chou Ta-Kuan's account of his time at Angkor, we know that Chinese visitors to the city were often outwitted in commercial transactions by local traders, a fact that Chou reports in a clearly peeved tone. But, overall, we are left having to be satisfied with the 'big picture', a situation that will not alter greatly until we are much closer to our present time.

The end of the classical age

Because so many changes took place in the thirteenth to fifteenth centuries, historians have asked whether there might have been a major identifiable event, or series of events, that could explain the downfall of the great states of classical times. Various suggestions have been put forward, including the activities of the Mongol dynasty, which caused the fall of Pagan, attempted to invade Java, and attacked Champa. Other 'single cause' explanations have pointed to the arrival of Theravada Buddhism, a more 'democratic' religion than Mahayana Buddhism and Hinduism, in the mainland of Southeast Asia, and of Islam in the maritime regions. And some have argued that a major cause of Angkor's fall was the spread of malaria as ruined canals provided an opportunity for mosquitoes to breed unchecked in stagnant water.

It seems probable that many, if not all, of these factors played some part over a period of more than two centuries as old states were no longer capable of adapting to different circumstances and new states emerged that proved better attuned to a changed world. But, importantly, the fact that the states of classical Southeast Asia passed from the scene did not mean that all of the values associated with those states disappeared. Quite to the contrary, the Southeast Asian world that emerged after the classical age owed a very great historical and cultural debt to earlier times.

2

Courts, kings and peasants: The traditional world

The fall of great empires and the abandonment of temple complexes did not signal an end to the traditions and cultural values that had dominated the lives of the rulers and their subjects. The empires and their greatness were not forgotten, and if we think of the classical period having come to an end in the fifteenth century, the values of that period lived on with remarkably little change for at least another three centuries. In some cases, these are values that still play a part in contemporary Southeast Asian life. Kings in the centuries that followed the classical period did not feel less royal or less important, though some may well have felt less powerful. The Southeast Asian world after the classical era was still essentially traditional in character, and this world did not begin to change in a notable fashion until the latter part of the eighteenth century. Since the Portuguese and Spanish established bases in Southeast Asia in the sixteenth century, with the

Dutch arriving at the beginning of the seventeenth, there is a need for an explanation why this was so. Why did the presence of these alien foreigners have remarkably little impact in the early decades of their presence?

The reason for nominating the eighteenth century as the time when traditional values began to come under challenge is simply explained. This was the century when Europeans slowly began to play an important role in determining the domestic politics of Southeast Asia. It was the last century in which the values of the traditional world were dominant, if not universal. Making the point another way, the eighteenth century witnessed a shift away from a situation in which most Southeast Asian states maintained an existence essentially untouched by the influence of Europe to one where it became impossible to ignore the European presence. Even so, much of the eighteenth century was a period of increasing confidence for many of the states of Southeast Asia. As examples of this confidence, there were important developments in literature in both Java and Vietnam. In Thailand, a new and dynamic royal dynasty, the Chakri, came to power in 1782. Its kings rebuilt the state following a devastating Burmese invasion in 1767 and reformed the legal system. Yet change of a momentous sort was looming over the region, for the nineteenth century was to witness the period of major European colonial expansion and with that expansion, a challenge to traditional values that Southeast Asians, both rulers and ruled, could not ignore.

A political mosaic: systems of government

If a cartographer were asked to make a political map of contemporary Southeast Asia, the result would show only ten states—eleven if East Timor is included. Undertaking the task for the region in the eighteenth century would be infinitely more complex; using different colours to show the boundaries of the various states by the use of different colours resulting in an extraordinary mosaic. It is difficult to even estimate how many colours would have to be used, but certainly no less than forty would be needed to show the existence of kingdoms, principalities, sultanates and lesser political units. Some of these minor eighteenth century states exercised control over no more than a few thousand people, with their very existence dependent on the goodwill of their larger neighbours. So a way would have to be found to distinguish between the states of real importance and those which led a precarious existence and which could be extinguished by a much more powerful overlord. But however the map was drawn up, it would have one distinctive feature—the areas showing a colonial presence would be very small indeed. Apart from the Spanish in the northern Philippine islands and the Dutch in parts of Java, the European presence in Southeast Asia at the end of the eighteenth century was extremely limited, made up of a few trading posts dotted along the coastlines of the various regions.

The bureaucracy of Vietnam

What sort of states existed in this still essentially traditional Southeast Asian world? The most distinctive was the Vietnamese state. During the eighteenth century, Vietnam was divided politically, first between two powerful families and in the last two decades of the century by a major rebellion. Nevertheless, all who contested power in Vietnam held to the ideal of a unified state in which Confucian values were dominant and the administration was modelled on that existing in China. This reliance on Chinese models, it should never be forgotten, did not mean that China was seen as having any right to interfere in Vietnam's internal affairs.

An important consequence of Vietnam's adoption of Chinese models was the theory, and to some extent the practice, that membership of the governing class was open to all comers who

A view of the Dutch colonial city of Batavia, on the northern coast of Java, in the early eighteenth century. Batavia, modern Jakarta, was well-placed to dominate sea traffic with the spice islands of eastern Indonesia, and it was the trade in spices that originally brought the Dutch to Indonesia. Built on low-lying ground, Batavia was a death trap for many of its European inhabitants, who succumbed to malaria or the consequences of appallingly inadequate sanitation. (PHOTOGRAPH FROM NATIONAL LIBRARY OF AUSTRALIA)

could meet the tests of scholarship. In an imperfect, but nevertheless important fashion, Vietnam was governed by what today would be called a 'meritocracy'. This was in great contrast to the Buddhist kingdoms of mainland Southeast Asia, and the traditional states of central Java, where officials formed a semi-hereditary class; being the son of an official was the vital fact that determined entry into the ranks of a ruler's administration. In Vietnam, the capacity to pass official exams was taken as the guiding principle, even if it often proved the case that the sons of officials had more opportunity to succeed in their studies and so to enter the official ranks.

Vietnamese officials advised a ruler who was spoken of as the 'Son of Heaven' and whose role was to mediate between the physical and the spiritual world by the correct observance of state and official ceremonies. Just as the performance of these ceremonies followed a minutely drawn-up set of procedures, so did the rest of Vietnamese official life involve following prescribed patterns of administrative behaviour. The bureaucracy was a pyramid with the ruler at the apex. Clearly defined links existed between the apex and the lowest level of officials in the provinces who formed the base of this administration. Vietnamese officials judged crimes according to a written legal code, detailed in form and complete with learned commentaries. Strict rules covered the amount of authority possessed by each grade of official, just as each level of official had a prescribed form of dress. And, unlike their neighbours who had not been influenced in the same way by China, the Vietnamese believed in the necessity of clearly defined borders showing the limits of the state.

In all these things, Vietnam was very different from the other major mainland states of Southeast Asia which had been influenced by Indian culture, and in particular, the Hindu and Buddhist

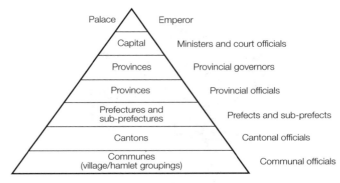

A schematic representation of the disposition of power in traditional Vietnamese society. Those occupying positions as officials below the level of prefects and sub-prefects were not members of Vietnam's mandarinate.

religions that had originated in the Indian sub-continent. Following the end of the classical period, the major states of mainland Southeast Asia were ruled by kings who had embraced Buddhism. In Burma, Thailand, Cambodia and the small states along the Mekong River that eventually came to form the country we know today as Laos, the influence of India in the courts of the region was less clear-cut than was the case with Chinese influence over Vietnam. For example, in Vietnam, officials dressed in essentially the same fashion as Chinese mandarins. With the exception of some court priests who dressed in the same fashion as Brahmins in India, such direct borrowing from India was not characteristic of the kingdoms of mainland Southeast Asia.

Vietnam is part of Southeast Asia, but culturally distinctively different through the influence of China. In traditional Vietnam this Chinese influence was visually apparent in the architecture of palaces and temples, and in the clothing of officials such as this high-ranking mandarin. (FROM *LE TOUR DU MONDE*, 1878)

Bending the rules in the Buddhist states

The organisation of the Buddhist states followed a very different pattern from that found in Vietnam. The pattern of official relationships was more complex, partly because it lacked the clear lines of authority found in Vietnam. Where the Vietnamese system aimed at controlling the state down to the level of the village, the central power in the Buddhist kingdoms followed a very different practice. Control over the more distant regions of the kingdom was readily delegated to provincial governors who were able to exercise almost unlimited power, always providing they did not challenge the king's position as the ultimate source of authority.

If a pyramid is a useful way to represent the manner in which Vietnam's traditional government operated, a series of concentric circles can represent the nature of power in the Buddhist kingdoms. The state would be contained within the largest of these concentric circles, but it was only at the centre, in the smallest circle, that the king's power was truly absolute. Beyond the central circle— beyond the limits of the palace, to take a real-life example—it was frequently the case that the king's power diminished in direct proportion to a region's distance from the capital. As for borders, the Buddhist rulers in mainland Southeast Asia accepted that these were uncertain and porous, something quite unthinkable for a Vietnamese official. The extent to which a particular area was seen as part of one state or another could vary according to circumstances, just as the populations in these areas might be regarded as under the authority of one ruler at one time, and a different ruler at another. As an example, the western provinces of modern Cambodia have, over the past two centuries, been ruled at various times as part of Thailand with sovereignty over this area changing hands on several occasions.

Kings, emperors and 'divine right'

The rulers of the Buddhist kingdoms were, as was the case with the Vietnamese emperor, expected to intercede between the world

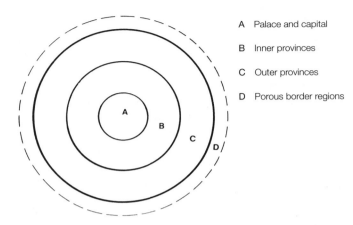

A   Palace and capital

B   Inner provinces

C   Outer provinces

D   Porous border regions

A schematic representation of the disposition of power in the traditional Buddhist states in mainland Southeast Asia. The more distant a region from the kingdom's capital, the less likely it was that the ruler exercised significant power there. Beyond the outer provinces, the border regions were porous, with uncertain boundaries.

of men and the spiritual world to ensure that the rains fell at the right time and were then followed by a dry season that brought crops to maturity. But there was a vital difference in the role of the Buddhist kings when compared with the Vietnamese emperor. In Thailand, and the other mainland Buddhist states, the king's status was semi-divine. The monarch and the throne he occupied were the centre of the kingdom, with monarchy as the linchpin that held the Buddhist kingdoms together. Despite his title as the 'Son of Heaven', the Vietnamese emperor did not have the same status. This is emphasised by the fact that for more than a hundred years, during the seventeenth and eighteenth centuries, the Vietnamese people were able to accept a situation in which their emperor was no more than a figurehead, a puppet at the beck and call of one of the two great families who were the real holders of power. However limited a king's power away from the capital in which he had his palace, and however much his senior officials might have tried to take advantage of a child succeeding to the throne, the idea of a state existing more as a reflection of its officials than of its ruler was not part of the system that existed in the Buddhist kingdoms.

Common to all of the Buddhist rulers of mainland Southeast Asia was a belief—held both by themselves and by their subjects— in their semi-divine or near-divine character. This semi-divine, magical role involved something more than the concept of 'divine right' associated with the Christian rulers of Europe. European rulers held an office, it was claimed, sanctioned by the Christian divinity. But no matter how elevated the status of European kings and princes, they were not semi-divine or nearly godlike themselves. Yet this is how the Buddhist kings were seen within their states. Their position as king was not only sanctioned by the Buddhist faith and continuing Hindu religious beliefs, they were removed from the rest of mankind and credited with possessing powers that only the divine, or near-divine, could hold.

This is the ideal picture and if the ideal had always prevailed there would never have been the family feuds, coups d'état, and all the other turbulent events that saw kings toppled from their thrones and ambitious men plotting to overthrow the monarch of the day. Yet if the reality was more complicated than the ideal, the ideal nevertheless remained of vital importance. Challengers who succeeded in removing a ruler from the throne immediately tried to claim all the semi-divine powers of the man they had defeated. The strength of the traditions described here are important for more modern history. The very important position occupied by the present King of Thailand is a reflection of the traditional, elevated status enjoyed by his predecessors. Traditional ideas of kingship also help to explain why, for many years, Norodom Sihanouk of Cambodia was able to reap great political advantage from the fact he had been Cambodia's king before abdicating his throne in 1955.

Royal figures have also been important in the recent history of the maritime regions of Southeast Asia. Unlike the rulers of the mainland kingdoms—again excluding Vietnam as a special case—the majority of the rulers of the states in the maritime world were followers of Islam, sultans who acted in the name of their religion as well as their state. As followers of Islam, they could not, in strict theory, be other than men, with the limitations that this involves. But, once again, strict theory was qualified, most particularly in those regions of the maritime world which had been influenced by Indian ideas—in parts of Indonesia and Malaysia.

Nowhere was this more true than in Java, where the rulers of the central Javanese kingdom of Mataram, which rose to power at the end of the sixteenth century, were followers of Islam. Just as importantly, perhaps even more importantly, they were inheritors of a rich mystical tradition drawing on Hindu-Buddhist ideas as well as an indigenous Javanese beliefs and values. The rulers of Mataram *were* more than men in a way that many of the sultans of the smaller states located along the coast and rivers of maritime Southeast Asia were not. These latter rulers had special rights and privileges, but they were men all the same. The ruler of Mataram gave formal acknowledgment to Islam, but the power that he exercised from within the walls of his *kraton* or palace was linked to mystical values. These values are better understood as similar to those of the Buddhist monarchs of the mainland than in terms of the authority held by the other traditional courts of island Southeast Asia. So while neither Sukarno nor Suharto, as presidents of Indonesia, were of royal descent, there is no doubt both benefited from the adoption, in their different ways, of styles of behaviour associated with traditional Javanese kingship.

Rulers and ruled in a single world

The gap between rulers and ruled in this traditional Southeast Asian world was profound. In traditional Vietnam it was possible for a talented peasant child to move into the ranks of the bureaucracy. But this was a rare event, and the division between rulers and ruled in the rest of the region was even more marked, so that moving into a higher social class only occurred in extraordinary times or could only be achieved by an extraordinary man.

The essential 'gap' or 'division' between ruler and ruled was that of power. Real power was in the hands of an elite few. There was no middle class in the traditional Southeast Asian world to moderate the stark division between ruler and ruled. This was a situation that contrasts sharply with the emergence of a middle class in European history. Yet there were differences among those who were ruled; in the world of the peasants, there were some who were clearly much better off materially than others. None were truly rich, but some had gained influence, and in terms of their immediate surroundings, a degree of power over others. This was not power matching that in the hands of the elite, but in a village context it set the better-off peasants apart from their fellows. These men and their families were community leaders and acted as go-betweens linking the village with higher authority. They were the final link between the distant court and the village.

Throughout Southeast Asia, the basic pattern of peasant life involved men and women assuring the right to farm land by the act of farming. Except in Vietnam, anything like the Western concept of land ownership did not exist. A family might work one area of land for generations, but the fields remained the 'property' of the ruler. This was an arrangement that posed few problems at a time when there was little pressure on land. And if circumstances, such as famine or war, made farming difficult in one area, peasants in traditional Southeast Asia were ready to move to another location, and so to place themselves under the authority of another ruler.

Life as a peasant was seldom easy and sometimes shockingly harsh. The risk of famine in countries that depended on monsoons to provide water for irrigating wet-rice cultivation was always in the background, for if the rains failed to fall, the prospect of starvation was real. In all but the poorest regions, there were occasions for village festivals with their accompanying gaiety, but these were exceptions to a way of life that was plagued by disease as well as demanding physical labour.

Although the peasant farmers were the largest group in the populations of traditional Southeast Asia outside of the elite ranks, there were other groups who should be mentioned. In larger

An engraving of a village house in Sumatra. The drawing from which this engraving was made was executed in 1792. Despite the slow increase in European contacts with Southeast Asia by the closing years of the eighteenth century, peasants, such as those seen in this picture, continued to live a life largely circumscribed by the limits of their village and its nearby regions. (FROM THE HISTORY OF SUMATRA, BY WILLIAM MARSDEN, PUBLISHED IN 1811, FROM NATIONAL LIBRARY OF AUSTRALIA)

villages and in the minor trading or administrative centres away from the great capitals, there were artisans and merchants. Along the coasts of both mainland and maritime Southeast Asia and on the rivers and lakes, there were fishermen whose occupation set them apart from the cultivators but who otherwise shared the same values and suffered similar hardships of life.

The world of the peasant, whether farmer or fisherman, of the artisan and the small trader was essentially a closed one. No truly autonomous villages existed, cut off from the world outside the village limits, but the links with the larger world were weak. The more prosperous villager might know a little of the regions beyond his rice fields, as the fisherman knew of the seas beyond the beach where he landed his catch and pulled his boat from the water. But the world beyond the village was only dimly perceived and the likelihood that anyone born into a village would leave it except during war or to live in another village was slim indeed. Above all, the basic reality of peasant life was the unchanging nature of existence.

Yet life was not necessarily static. Not only did villagers move from their homes in the face of famine or to avoid war, itinerant traders travelled with their caravans right across the face of mainland Southeast Asia, reaching from Burma into the highland regions of modern Vietnam. Indonesian traders from Sumatra, the northern ports of Java and Sulawesi crisscrossed the seas of the Archipelago on their voyages. Yet having ventured abroad, they returned to a world that altered little from year to year and decade to decade.

Despite the divide between ruled and elite, it was still the case that these two groups lived in a single, unified world. The courts and kings were separate from the farmers, fishermen and petty traders over whom they ruled, but just as the serf and feudal lord of medieval Europe both sensed themselves to be part of Christendom, so the peasants and fishermen sensed themselves as being within the same world as their ruler, whether he was an Islamic sultan, a Buddhist king or a Vietnamese Confucian emperor. This was a sense that was to alter with the growing power of Europeans as these newcomers brought unstoppable change to the region. But, at the beginning, the Europeans were far from exerting the kind of overwhelming power they later displayed.

The Europeans arrive: early influences

In a world united by instant telecommunications, so that events in the most isolated of regions can be beamed instantly on to distant television sets by way of satellites, it is difficult to imagine a time when the Southeast Asian region was unknown to Europe. Yet this was the case until the thirteenth century, for it was not until then that the first European contact was made with Southeast Asia, by Marco Polo. In very recent times, there have been suggestions that this famed Venetian traveller did not, in fact, go to China, so that his account of life there and of his travels through Southeast Asia were a giant literary fraud. Majority opinion still thinks that Polo did, indeed, travel as he claimed, so that we can accept as largely truthful his tantalisingly incomplete references to having passed both through Burma, in the course of overland travel to Bengal, and the account of his voyage home that took him through the Indonesian Archipelago. Much less well-known than Marco Polo was another early visitor, the Italian Franciscan friar, Odoric of Pordenone, who travelled through Southeast Asia in the first half of the fourteenth century. Like Polo, he left an account of his travels, and like Polo, his solitary voyaging had no impact on the countries through which he passed. Another century was to pass before there was any European impact on the countries of Southeast Asia, when the Iberians, Portuguese and Spanish founded their outposts in the East.

Yet how important was the impact of the Portuguese, who captured the great trading city of Malacca, on the west coast of peninsular Malaysia, in 1511, and the Spaniards whose early contacts with the Philippine islands, begun by Magellan in 1521, led to the capture of Manila in 1571? There is no doubt that, in the past, too much importance was accorded the actions of the Europeans. Of course, the fall of Malacca to the Portuguese was important for the men and women who lived there and for the merchants involved in the spice trade which had brought the Portuguese to Southeast Asia. And, in the case of the Philippines, the arrival of the Spanish had particularly important effects in shaping the nature of colonial and post-colonial Philippines society. Not least, the Spanish in the Philippines eventually succeeded in making it the only country in Southeast Asia with Christianity as the dominant religion.

Although first on the scene, the Portuguese were ultimately unable to counter the power and energy of their Dutch competitors, so that in the end they maintained no more than a remote presence in the eastern part of Timor, the modern East Timor that has had such a tragic recent history. Their competitors, the Dutch, who lived, and usually after a very short time, died in Indonesia, were important indeed for the merchants in the ports of the Netherlands, as they developed a commercial system that for a period brought great profit to the Dutch state and its merchants. But the impact of the Dutch outside their base in Java, Batavia (modern Jakarta), and their outposts scattered through the islands, was restricted until the middle, or even the end, of the eighteenth century. A similar comment cannot be made about the Spaniards in the Philippines.

The Spanish and the Philippines: a special case

In general terms, the Spanish came to an area of Southeast Asia in which no central authority exercised power over the many small communities that were scattered along the coasts of the Philippine islands or in their interior. There were some exceptions in the southern islands of the Philippines, however. Here, the adoption of Islam by traditional leaders had helped them to organise states

The Spanish established their colonial headquaters for the Philippines in Manila in 1571. By the mid-seventeenth century Manila, as seen in this engraving, was a substantial town. Trade was Manila's lifeblood. Silver and gold from the Americas was exchanged for goods brought to Manila from East Asia, with the commerce handled by Manila's large resident Chinese population. Power, however, was firmly in the hands of the Spanish, with the State and Catholic Church working hand-in-hand to further political control and the conversion of the population.

that used the unifying force of religion to incorporate a number of communities into a single political unit. By the middle of the sixteenth century, Islam was slowly gaining ground in the more northerly islands and had reached as far as Manila. But this was very much a coastal phenomenon and the inland areas remained untouched by the new religion, so that the Spaniards encountered a society in which a large village was the essential unit. Authority, as elsewhere in Southeast Asia, rested in the hands of a headman who, through birth and inheritance, or through ability, was more prosperous than his fellow villagers.

The absence of central power in the northern Philippines (for the southern islands were never to experience significant Spanish rule, apart from a few port centres), enabled the Spanish colonisers to implant themselves in a way unmatched anywhere else in Southeast Asia. And unlike anywhere else in the region, the principal agents for the Spanish advance were not soldiers or traders but missionary priests. Missionaries played important roles elsewhere, particularly in Vietnam, but what occurred in the Philippines was unique. For, in the Philippines, the church and the state were inseparable, as they were in other areas of the world that fell under Spanish colonial control. Indeed, anyone seeking insights into the nature of the colonial period in the Philippines, may be better served looking at the Spanish experience in Latin America than at what happened in Southeast Asia.

The impact of Spanish values, particularly Spanish Christian values, on the peasant society of the Philippines was profound. The Philippines became the one country in Southeast Asia in which Christianity became more than a minority religion. In a slow but ultimately effective fashion, the combined force of the church and the state shaped the nature of rural society in the Philippines. New and greater power was given to traditional leaders, but beyond the village or district level, power was firmly in the hands of the Spanish. Yet while this led to the emergence of an educated Philippine class that resented Spanish political control, it also laid the foundations for a rural economy. Centuries of colonial control developed, strengthened and gave legitimacy to the high degree of social stratification that still remains a feature of Philippine life. Above all, the colonial society that developed in the Philippines was marked by land held by the few, with the majority of the rural population working either as tenant farmers or, more usually as very poor day labourers.

Changes that preceded the colonial advance

When, in the nineteenth century, European colonialism brought change to the rest of Southeast Asia, including Thailand (despite its never having experienced colonial occupation), it was the elite members of local societies who first bore the brunt of a changed political order. Yet these elites had already been experiencing and inspiring change themselves, before the colonial advance. The last three decades of the eighteenth century in Vietnam were marked by political upheaval and by challenges to established social and economic patterns as the result of a major rebellion. This rebellion was then followed by the emergence of a vigorous new dynasty that united all of Vietnam under its rule. Similarly, in Thailand, the advent of the new Chakri dynasty after 1782 brought a remarkable series of kings to power. They were men whose energies transformed the state. In the courts of central Java the late eighteenth century was a time of great literary achievement. And in the early nineteenth century Nguyen Du (1765–1820), who was regarded as Vietnam's greatest poet, wrote the most famous of all Vietnamese epic poems, the *Kim Van Kieu*. 'The Tale of Kieu' tells the story of selfless love and devotion to family, with the heroine, Kieu, the ideal model of Confucian values. At one stage, having to choose between her loved one, Kim, and her family, she knows she must choose the latter.

> By what means could she save her flesh and bone?
> When evil strikes, you bow to circumstance.
> And you must weigh and choose between your love
> and filial duty, which will turn the scale?
> She put aside all vows of love and troth—
> a child first pays the debts of birth and care.
>
> (HUYNH SANH THONG, TRANSLATOR, *THE TALE OF KIEU*, 1983)

At the end of the poem, after being forced to live as a concubine, Kieu is reunited with her family and Kim. But she and Kim never live together as man and wife.

These developments had little meaning for the peasants who lived in a world that went on as before, with life dominated by the cycle of crop planting and harvest, the seasons of the year, and the awesome events of birth and death. Visualising their physical world in the eighteenth century is difficult in the extreme. The present offers only limited insights into their past, while entering their spiritual world is even more difficult, perhaps impossible. At best, we may sense something of the complexity of this spiritual world where animistic beliefs blended with one or other of the great religions or philosophies—Islam, Buddhism, Hinduism, Confucianism or Christianity. For even the most sympathetic latter-day observer can only penetrate a certain distance into the religious world of another culture in another age.

Dramatic change was coming which would affect Southeast Asian societies at all levels. But before charting the advance of the European colonial powers and the challenge to traditional society that they represented, there was another element in the world that existed before colonialism that needs to be described. This was the presence within traditional society of minorities and slaves, the outsiders in traditional Southeast Asia.

3

Minorities and slaves: Outsiders in traditional Southeast Asia

For the rulers and the ruled of traditional Southeast Asia, there was a sense of belonging to a single world, a world defined by a shared religion and the acceptance of a monarch whose legitimacy was beyond question. But not everyone in this traditional world belonged, in the sense of being a member of the dominant ethnic group within the state. There were, it's true, a small number of immigrants, or their descendants, from distant regions—Indians, Persians, Chinese and Arabs who lived in the region but were not 'part' of it. They, too, did not belong, but, until the late nineteenth century, and with the notable exception of the large immigrant Chinese community in colonial Batavia (modern Jakarta), these immigrant minority groups were not really important. For mainland Southeast Asia, and to a much lesser extent in the maritime regions, the true outsiders in the traditional world were the people living in the hills and mountains.

Hill and valley: divided societies

The 'hill–valley' division of traditional Southeast Asian society was of a different order from the division between ruler and ruled in the ethnically unified mainland states. The lowland peasant farmer was part of the dominant society, if only a very humble part. In contrast, the people who lived in upland regions were a group for whom the administrative apparatus of the lowland state had little meaning. Above all, these hill peoples did not share the values of lowland society.

The number and variety of minority groups in the upland regions of mainland Southeast Asia were considerable. So too were their levels of development when compared with those of lowland society. In traditional Southeast Asia, many of the hill people were nomadic farmers who practised slash and burn agriculture—'eating the forest', in their own striking phrase. They levelled and burned trees, and found in the resulting ash a temporarily highly fertile site for planting crops. Others were members of fixed societies, farming in the high valleys in which they lived, using wet-rice techniques, but largely remaining apart from the lives of those who lived on the plains.

The ethnic and linguistic links between the people of the hills and those of the valleys were often close, if frequently un-recognised. While sections of the great Tai-speaking ethnic groups preferred to remain in their mountain valleys rather than join their linguistic cousins in the plains, they were aware of their common basic language, hence they called themselves Tai. Others, such as Sedang and Bahnar hill people living in the mountains that run between Vietnam and Cambodia, spoke a language linked to Khmer or Cambodian but had no sense of a shared ethnic identity with the people who spoke a similar language in the lowlands.

The essential division between the two groups was the almost total lack of any sense of *social* identity between them. Whatever the links that sometimes brought the two groups into contact, there was a near-absolute social division. This division was summed up in the words chosen by the dominant lowland societies to describe the peoples of the hills. The words were disparaging and disdainful, emphasising the unbridgeable social and cultural gap separating the two groups. Uplanders were *moi* to the Vietnamese, *phnong* to the Cambodians, and *kha* to the Lao. All these words can be translated as 'savage' or 'barbarian', fitting well with Rudyard Kipling's concept of 'lesser breeds without the law'.

Yet this deep social and cultural division did not mean there was no contact between dominant and non-dominant groups. Despised they might be, but it was the people in the hills who had the knowledge to aid a lowland army wishing to move across the hills and mountains to strike at an enemy. And who else could guide the slave-raiding parties from the lowlands to the most remote regions and aid in the capture of men, women and children whose primitive societies set them furthest apart from those dwelling on the plains?

Until very recently, lowland governments have not generally found it necessary to become involved in the day-to-day affairs of upland areas. Provided the populations of those areas did not act against the interests of the state, then they were free to govern themselves. In some of the mountainous areas of northern Thailand, for instance, it was only in the 1960s that the Bangkok government established a police presence. Such a policy was only possible where the upland peoples were regarded as posing no threat to the government and populations of the plains. This was not how matters stood in Burma, where relations between lowland ethnic Burmans and the country's indigenous minorities were of a quite different order.

Burma as a special case

In the mainland states of traditional Southeast Asia—Cambodia, Thailand and Vietnam, and with some qualifications, Laos—there were clearly dominant ethnic groups: Cambodians (Khmers),

Thais, Vietnamese and Lao. The situation was different elsewhere: in Burma on the mainland and in maritime Southeast Asia. On the mainland, Burma stood out in sharp contrast to its neighbours. Despite its long history, Burma has seldom been a unified state. Ethnic Burmans have dominated the major river valleys, but the populations of the upland regions that fall within Burma's frontiers have readily accepted the governments the Burmans have sought to impose on them. Indeed, from the first recorded history of Burma to the present day, tensions between the different ethnic groups and the Burmans have been a continuing problem. This is because of the large size of Burma's indigenous minorities. The Shans, Kachins, Karens and Chins, to mention only the most prominent of the non-Burman groups, make up approximately one third of the entire population—the Shans and Karens alone account for something like 16 per cent of Burma's total population.

Minorities of this size underline the much greater ethnic unity of Thailand, Cambodia and Vietnam. In each of these countries, the indigenous minorities are less than 15 per cent of the total population. If the indigenous minorities of these three countries may be described as outsiders, the term takes on a different meaning in relation to Burma. There, the Shans, Karens and others were outsiders too, but outsiders who again and again showed themselves ready to resist attempts by the Burmans to impose their will upon them. This is a situation that has continued into the present day, when finding a way to deal with the country's minorities remains a major problem for the government in Rangoon (now officially Yangon).

Fragmented coastal populations

What has just been described for mainland Southeast Asia had no real parallel in the maritime regions. Although the inhabitants of the traditional maritime world, from the Malayan Peninsula to

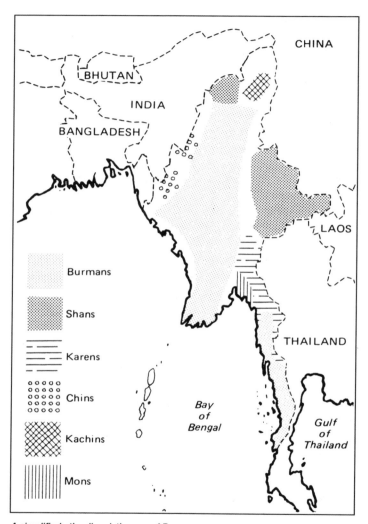

A simplified ethnolinguistic map of Burma
Among the countries of mainland Southeast Asia, Burma is distinctive because of the high proportion of ethnic minorities within its borders. More than 30 per cent of Burma's population is made up of minority groups.

the Philippine islands, spoke a series of languages that have a common linguistic root, the geographical character of their environment, with thousands of islands separated by sea, encouraged fragmentation rather than unity. Only in Java, during traditional times, were sizeable land-based states able to establish themselves. Instead of there being a pattern of dominant majorities and non-dominant minorities, the population of the maritime world is much better seen as composed of an intricately related series of ethnic groups. Only rarely was there a situation in which one clearly defined ethnic group dominated another minority group. Rather, territory was associated with groups of people who had a clear picture of their own identity and their separateness from others. This was true whether one talks of the Bugis seafarers of Sulawesi, the Sundanese of West Java or the Dayak tribesmen of the interior of Borneo. In the geographically fragmented and often environmentally difficult world of maritime Southeast Asia, the establishment of large states was mostly impossible and the survival of smaller states and of many tribal areas was common.

There were, and are, some limited examples of primitive hill populations whose level of development set them apart from the larger ethnic groups of the maritime world. Found in scattered groups, from the Malayan Peninsula through to the Indonesian Archipelago and the Philippine islands, are the descendants of some of the earliest inhabitants of the region. Always small in numbers and described as 'negritos' by ethnographers, they have never represented a challenge to the other, larger ethnic groups who live in the lowlands.

The real division in the maritime world was not between hill and valley dweller, but between those who followed a pattern of life linked to a permanent base, whether for farming, fishing or trading, and those who pursued a nomadic life combining hunting with slash-and-burn agriculture. In the mainland world, the nomadic cultivator was, of necessity, an uplander, but this was not the case in maritime Southeast Asia. As far as most of the nomadic or semi-nomadic groups of the traditional maritime world were concerned, they were not linked in any way to the state systems of more settled peoples. The Iban, or Sea Dayaks, of modern Sarawak on the island of Borneo are a classic example of such a group.

'Slavery' in traditional Southeast Asia

From the earliest accounts of Southeast Asia written by European visitors to the region there are references to the presence of 'slaves'. It's clear that there were, indeed, men, women and children who, from a Western point of view, lived in the deplorable conditions that are usually associated with the word 'slave'. These were true outsiders, persons who could never share in the benefits of the societies in which they laboured. They were the property of their

When the French Mekong River expedition passed through Stung Treng in northeastern Cambodia in 1866 its members observed minority hill peoples being sold into slavery. The expedition's artist recorded the faces of some of these hill people, who lived very different lives from the dominant lowland Cambodians.

owners, to be treated and disposed of as their owners pleased; there was no hope of release for them or their children, who were automatically slaves from birth. Prisoners of war and persons seized in slaving expeditions most usually filled this unenviable role.

In his book, *Voyage d'exploration en Indo-Chine*, published in 1885, the French explorer, Francis Garnier, gave an account of slaves he saw in Stung Treng, located in the northeast of modern Cambodia, in 1866. It was, he noted, a 'profitable trade'.

> . . . I saw, a few months later, the arrival in Stung Treng of a convoy of slaves and I could not help being deeply moved by this sight. While the men appeared to be largely indifferent to their fate, the women grasped their young children to them in an agitated manner, hiding them in their arms with their eyes showing their agonised fear every time someone came to look at them.

Yet European observers often failed to recognise that there were others whom they called slaves who did not really merit the description. Western visitors to the traditional world of Southeast Asia seldom understood the difference between 'true' slaves, condemned to a life of unending servitude, and persons who had voluntarily, but temporarily, given up their freedom to meet a debt or other unfilled obligation. These debt bondsmen were not outsiders in the true sense, though clearly the treatment they received from their masters varied greatly from place to place and period to period.

Finally, and giving emphasis to the complex nature of traditional Southeast Asia, there were other groups of persons who occupied indeterminate positions as hereditary servants of great rulers or officials. They were people such as the court servants in the *kratons* of the rulers of central Javanese states, or the elephant grooms for the kings of Thailand and Cambodia. They did not live outside the societies in which they performed their tasks, and they had no choice in their occupation—their position in life and the duties they performed each day were pre-ordained by birth.

Outsiders from the West

The outsiders described so far lived in a traditional world that placed a high value on order, on the observance of proper procedures, and on each strata of society knowing its proper place. With its deep respect for traditional practices, it was also a world that was vulnerable to the efforts of those who were not Southeast Asians to change it. For when the men of the West came to the region in numbers that were sufficient to challenge the traditional order, they frequently did not play by the rules Southeast Asians understood. Even when these Western newcomers thought they were doing so, this was seldom really the case. The resultant change was often as great as if deliberate attempts had been made to introduce new ideas and techniques.

The traditional Southeast Asian world of the eighteenth century may have been one that felt it had the answers to its own problems, whether these were of peace and war, the relationship of man to the universe and the gods that controlled it, or the need to find proper patterns of behaviour towards different groups inside and outside society. These were no longer the only problems that had to be faced as the West increasingly affected the daily life of an ever-growing number of Southeast Asians. Some of the answers Southeast Asians found to the new challenges they confronted were the result of a conscious search for solutions. Some of the problems have never been fully answered. Challenge became the keynote of the nineteenth and twentieth centuries—challenge to traditional ways of exercising political power, to the acceptance of traditional values, and to the traditional pattern of economic life. As these challenges developed, so was the traditional Southeast Asian world slowly but steadily undermined.

4

The challenge of the West: The European advance

Ever since the Second World War, historians have debated how much importance should be given to the role of Europe and Europeans in the modern history of Southeast Asia. These debates have not ended, but it's fair to say that there are now some broad areas of agreement about the issue. Most importantly, there is an acknowledgment that in the past too much attention has been given to the role of the Europeans —to the exclusion of the part played by Southeast Asians in their own history. And hand in hand with this conclusion has been a recognition that some older histories of the region as a whole, and of individual countries, were quite misleading in the historical picture they presented. The way in which Indonesia's history was once presented provides a notable example of this outdated approach.

Before the Second World War, and even after, it was quite common for history books to refer to the Dutch having ruled over the Indonesian islands for hundreds of years. The Dutch had arrived in Java in the seventeenth century and so, general histories often suggested, these islands had been a Dutch colony for three hundred years. The errors of such a picture are glaring, but it was a picture that had wide acceptance—in Europe, at least. The idea of the whole of Indonesia having been a Dutch colony for three hundred years takes no account of the fact that large areas of modern-day Indonesia did not come under Dutch control until the late nineteenth century and even later. Bali, to take the example of one of the areas of Indonesia best known to foreigners, was not finally brought under Dutch control until after a short but singularly bloody battle in Denpasar, the island's modern administrative capital, in 1906.

Readjusting the lens through which we look at Southeast Asia's history to take account of the rich and important role of its peoples does not, of course, mean that the role of Europeans and of Western colonialism can be ignored. Quite to the contrary, for the period of colonialism in the nineteenth and twentieth century was clearly of great importance. What is different about histories written today, in contrast to those written forty or fifty years ago is a matter of balance. And seeking to provide a more balanced picture certainly takes account of the European role, even if in a rather different fashion than once was the case.

Writing about Indonesia's history must take account of the Dutch. The Dutch in Indonesia, as was the case for the Spaniards and Americans in the Philippines, the French in the countries of Indochina, and the British in Burma and Malaya, were important participants in the historical developments of all of these countries. In some aspects of history, the role played by Europeans was vital in determining developments of far-reaching significance. The establishment of international boundaries was one such case. In other aspects of life, the part played by Europeans was much less important than it was once thought to have been. Before the Second World War, French commentators confidently wrote of the way in which the colonial administration in Vietnam was implanting French culture in the colonised population. This was never true for the majority of the Vietnamese population. French language and culture, all French claims to the contrary, never became a substitute for indigenous values and the Vietnamese language.

Looking at the period of European colonialism in a balanced fashion, we still have to ask the question, 'What did the Europeans achieve as they asserted their political and economic control over Southeast Asia?' At the most fundamental level, the answer to this question would seem to be that the Europeans as colonialists became, for a period, the dominant powers of the region. As they established the colonial boundaries that have become, with minor exceptions, the borders of the independent states of Southeast Asia, the Europeans called into question old values and ways of conducting government. In imposing their control over the countries of the region, the Europeans revealed the inadequacies of past systems. An understanding of these political developments and the shifts in power that were involved is best gained by examining what happened on a country-by-country basis as the establishment of colonial rule ended forever the traditional world that has been described in previous chapters.

The mainland states

European expansion into the states of mainland Southeast Asia was a nineteenth century development in contrast to the much earlier association of the Dutch with Indonesia and the Spanish with the Philippines. The first major advance was by the British into Burma.

Burma

Until the end of the eighteenth century, Burma had not been a target of major European expansion. Plagued over the centuries by chronic problems of ethnic disunity, Burma in the eighteenth century seemed to have found a new lease of life under the Konbaung dynasty. Two vigorous leaders, Alaungpaya (reigned 1752–60) and most particularly Bodawpaya (reigned 1782–1819), imposed a measure of internal unity while confronting and containing external threats to the state. By the end of the eighteenth century, there was a new and different threat to be faced—the slow expansion of British power into areas of northeastern India, areas that Burmese rulers had long regarded as falling within their sphere of influence.

Here was a textbook case of a clash between alien and Southeast Asian values. Burmese rulers regarded the regions of Assam, Manipur and Arakan lying in or near to the west of modern Burma as a frontier zone in which their interests should prevail. They expected that Burmese interests should be paramount and that there should be no place for others to challenge those interests. This was quite opposite to the view held by the officials of the British East India Company, whose power was expanding into northeastern India. The idea of a frontier zone without clear boundaries was unacceptable to them, as was the view of the Burmese court that it was not responsible for the actions of the petty rulers over whom Burma claimed paramountcy—so long as these actions did not harm Burmese interests. If, the British argued, raiding parties from Assam, Manipur or Arakan struck into territories under East India Company control, then the Burmese court was responsible and should act to prevent its 'subjects' from behaving in this way.

There was no meeting of minds on this issue, and there were other factors irritating the British. Burmese treatment of British traders and disagreements over how diplomatic exchanges should be carried out between the Burmese and the British steadily poisoned relations. Then finally, and fatally for the Burmese, Burma's ruler, King Bagyidaw (reigned 1819–37) chose to confront the British by invading Bengal, an area of India firmly under British control. In response, the British advanced into Burma, captured Rangoon and imposed the Treaty of Yandabao in 1826 that gave the East India Company control of Arakan and Tenasserim, the coastal regions of modern Burma running along the Bay of Bengal and the Andaman Sea.

This was the extent of Britain's advance for some twenty years, but once again a confrontation took place which showed there was no meeting of minds between the Burmese and the British. This time, trade and prestige were at the heart of the clash between the two sides. By the early 1850s, British traders in Rangoon were growing increasingly resentful of their treatment by the Burmese officials in that city. Regarding the British merchants as interlopers, the Burmese also saw them as fair game for personal enrichment. So they persecuted the alien merchants, subjecting them to all manner of extortion. In behaving in this way, the officials believed that Burmese prestige was enhanced; it demonstrated unassailable Burmese power. This judgment, coming as it did at a time of increased colonial rivalry among the European powers, proved fatally wrong. The British came to see events in Burma as a test of strength for their role in East Asia as a whole. At first without authorisation, but later with approval from London, British troops fought the Second Burma War (1852–53) that led to the occupation of Lower Burma, an area of agricultural and timber wealth.

The final British advance, which led to their occupation of the whole of Burma after the Third Burma War in 1885, was a reflection of two broad themes—the chronic domestic weaknesses of the Burmese court and the now intense imperial rivalry between Britain and France in mainland Southeast Asia. Plagued by internal squabbling, the Burmese court seems never to have realised how perilous its position was. At the same time, its officials continued to see foreign traders as a target for personal enrichment through extortion. As for the British, by the 1880s Burma was not simply important as a potential source of wealth, it was also an element in their rivalry with France for spheres of influence in Asia. By 1886, Britain had captured the Burmese capital of

Mandalay and proclaimed control over those areas of Burma not previously occupied. 'British Burma' had come into existence and a firm border was fixed between Burma and India. Harsh though the judgment may seem, as prisoners of their own view of the world, the Burmese leaders were unable to see that the values to which they attached so much importance were meaningless to the British. Burma was to remain under British rule until 1948.

Vietnam

Like Burma, Vietnam came under colonial control in a series of steps. But unlike Burma, the imposition of French rule was completed in twenty-five years rather than nearly sixty. And in a fashion similar to Burma, also, Vietnam's ruler and court behaved in a way that suggested they had no real understanding of the challenge posed by the French.

At first glance, Vietnam in the 1850s seemed an unlikely candidate to fall under colonial control. United under a single ruler in 1802, the country seemed set on a path for success, whatever internal difficulties had to be overcome. A small number of voices within the Vietnamese court at Hue warned of the dangers that could be posed by expanding European powers, but they were disregarded.

The French saw Vietnam as a springboard for trade with China, little realising that Vietnam's geographic position next to China did not mean that any major trade passed between the two countries. When, in 1858, French forces invaded Vietnam—having pledged to protect Christian missionaries and jealous of British colonial expansion elsewhere—the Vietnamese court could scarcely believe what was happening. The Confucian order that guided their lives had not prepared the ruler and his officials for this grave development. Once they found that they could not repel the invading French by force, the Vietnamese adopted a policy which had little more than hope as its justification. With the French occupying a large, fertile area in southern Vietnam between 1859

By comparison with the rulers of other traditional states of Southeast Asia, the Vietnamese emperors differed in maintaining a standing army. The existence of this army, and a belief in the power of their Confucian ideology, misled the Vietnamese rulers and their officials into thinking they could withstand the onslaught of French colonisation. In the event, soldiers such as those shown here were no match for the much better armed French soldiers who gradually conquered the whole of Vietnam between 1858 and 1886. (FROM *LE TOUR DU MONDE*, 1878)

and 1867, the Vietnamese in the court at Hue hoped the invaders would advance no further, even if they did not go away.

Their hopes were futile. The French were determined to stay and in the 1880s proceeded to extend their colonial possessions to include all of Vietnam. By doing so, the French did more than establish a new colonial empire in the East. They also accelerated the developing intellectual crisis in Vietnam. The powerful conservative faction in the Vietnamese court which had disregarded the warnings of those who had pointed to the threatening power of the West was now shown to have been dreadfully wrong. From this point on, new Vietnamese voices were raised that sought to come to terms with what had happened.

The French did not determine the geographical shape of Vietnam as was the case with colonial rule in other parts of Southeast Asia. Neither did they create a state where none had existed before, unlike what happened in the the maritime regions. But by invading Vietnam and then imposing an alien government, the French played a vital part in the destruction of the old Vietnamese order. In their subsequent unreadiness to share power with the Vietnamese and to consider the possibility of independence for their colony, the French did more: they set the stage for one of the most powerful revolutions in Southeast Asia's history.

Cambodia

By comparison with Burma and Vietnam, Cambodia was a minor state in the mainland Southeast Asian world. Little remained of its former greatness, and even its magnificent temple ruins had, by the middle of the nineteenth century, passed out of Cambodian control to lie within the territories of the King of Thailand. That Cambodia survived at all, located as it was between the expanding power of Thailand and Vietnam, was a reflection of the unreadiness of the rulers of those two much more powerful states to push their rivalry to its ultimate conclusion. They concluded that their interests would best be served by permitting Cambodia's continued existence as a buffer zone between them.

The decision of the French to extend control over Cambodia, beginning in the 1860s, ensured the state's survival. And not only the state's, for, by treating the Cambodian king, Norodom I, in such a way that he remained as the symbolic leader of the nation the French also boosted the prestige of the royal family and the officials associated with the court. This policy contrasted sharply with what happened in both Burma and Vietnam. In each of those countries, the colonial power—Britain in Burma, France in

King Norodom as a young man in 1859 before he gained the throne. (FROM *LE TOUR DU MONDE*, 1863.)

Vietnam—followed policies that undermined the prestige and symbolic authority of the ruler. In Cambodia, both as the result of planning and lack of it, the French helped the traditional royal leadership to remain important politically.

Laos

The country that we know as Laos did not exist in the nineteenth century. Its modern territorial area was occupied by a confusing pattern of minor states, none of them able to act in any truly independent fashion. In the traditional Southeast Asian manner, these petty states were linked to larger, more powerful neighbours. In European terminology, they were the vassals of more powerful suzerains, some to Thailand, some to Burma and some to China. In some cases, a state was the vassal of more than one suzerain.

The fact that Laos came into existence was the result of colonial rivalry. As the nineteenth century drew to a close, rivalry between France and Britain on the Southeast Asian mainland was intense. With the British established in Burma and the French controlling Vietnam and Cambodia, the question of where spheres of influence would lie was a matter for prolonged debate. Finally, with Thailand having to make concessions to Western interests but able to preserve its independence, the French and British concluded that it was in their interest to maintain Thailand as a buffer state between their colonial possessions.

What was possible for Thailand was denied the Lao states. Without unity of their own, being the vassals of various overlords, and subject to increasing disorder as Chinese refugees and bandits spilled out of China into the region below China's southern border, the Lao states appeared an attractive prospect for colonial advance. The opportunity was seized by the French between 1887 and 1899. Through a combination of individual audacity, great power manoeuvring, and a reliance on dubious claims linked to Vietnam's past suzerainty over sections of Laos, the French established a colonial position in Laos. More clearly than anywhere else in mainland Southeast Asia, this was a case of the European colonial advance bringing into existence a new state, one that despite great political transformations has survived to the present day.

Thailand

Despite its success in avoiding the experience of colonial control, Thailand, too, was affected by the great changes that accompanied the colonial advance in the rest of Southeast Asia. Along with Vietnam, Thailand was one of the two notably successful states of Southeast Asia, and was still growing in strength in the first half of the nineteenth century. The fact that it was able to avoid becoming a colony was a reflection of many factors, not least that it was seen by both Britain and France as a useful buffer zone between their colonial possessions in Burma and the Indochinese countries. But there were more positive reasons for the Thai achievement, the most important being that Thailand enjoyed the leadership of remarkable kings and officials.

The contrast between Thailand and Burma in this regard is particularly striking. Facing a new and alien threat from the British, Burma's Buddhist kings and officials found it almost impossible to appreciate the nature of the challenge, let alone to think of ways of resisting it. In Thailand, on the other hand, inquiring minds from the king downwards were already seeking to understand the nature of European power and the scientific and technical learning that went with it.

King Mongkut (reigned 1851–68), a man sadly misrepresented in the popular musical *The King and I*, was one of the most important of all Thai rulers and a vitally important architect of Thailand's plans for avoiding foreign rule. His strategies involved positive efforts to acquire Western knowledge and diplomatic concessions that prevented an opportunity arising that could be used by one or other of the European powers as an excuse to impose foreign rule. His approach was followed by his successor, King Chulalongkorn (reigned 1868–1910). What is more, both these remarkable kings were served by able senior associates, either members of the royal family or officials in the Thai court.

Yet the challenges of the European powers could not be evaded entirely. French determination to consolidate their colonial position in the Indochinese region led to Thailand losing its suzerainty over territories along the Mekong River and over the western provinces of Cambodia that had been administered as part of Thailand for over a century. These losses of Thai territory took place at the end of the nineteenth century. A little later, in 1909, Thailand conceded control over four southern Malay states to the British. These states—Perlis, Kedah, Kelantan and Trengganu— then became associated with the British colonial empire in the Malayan Peninsula and form part of the modern state of Malaysia.

So while Thailand never became a colony it was very much affected by the colonial advance. And it not only lost territory; it also had to make substantial concessions to foreign interests within its own boundaries. For instance, the Thais had to allow European foreigners to be granted extraterritorial legal status, meaning that a European foreigner accused of a crime was not tried by Thai courts but by special tribunals staffed by foreigners. Yet despite these facts, Thailand presented a singular contrast to the rest of Southeast Asia. Thai leaders followed policies that revealed a remarkable capacity to gain the greatest benefit from the new and intrusive elements of European power. These policies included seeking to gain the benefits of modern science and technology through the employment of foreign, European advisers.

The maritime states

The European advance into the states of maritime Southest Asia began in the sixteenth century with the Portuguese capture of Malacca. By the early seventeenth century the Dutch were active in parts of Indonesia and the Spanish had established colonial bridgeheads in the Philippines. Nevertheless, it is important to remember that the degree of influence these alien powers exerted over the political life of the region was limited in the extreme.

Indonesia

In mainland Southeast Asia, the colonial powers established their control over a period of some sixty years. But in the case of Indonesia, it took the Dutch over three hundred years to put in place an empire stretching across the archipelago, with the greatest Dutch advance taking place over a period of some sixteen years at the end of the nineteenth century.

The Dutch came to the Indonesian Archipelago as traders. To pursue their initial goals it was enough to gain control of the major ports of northern Java and the principal commercial centres of the eastern islands linked to the spice trade. Slowly, and in a fashion similar to what happened with the British in India, the Dutch East India Company became as much a territorial power as a trading operation. When internal rivalries led to the collapse of the central Javanese kingdom of Mataram in the eighteenth century, the Dutch were already involved in manipulating local politics and were vitally interested in playing a part in overseeing the establishment of Mataram's successor states based in the central Javanese capitals of Yogyakarta and Surakarta (Solo).

At the beginning of their time as colonialists, the Dutch made great profits through their trade in Indonesia. This was reflected in their extravagant lifestyle that went hand in hand with a high rate of death from tropical disease. John Barrow, an English official who visited Batavia (Jakarta) in 1792, wrote as a critic when he described the colonial Dutch at breakfast:

> . . . the Dutchman . . . lives to eat, rather than eats to live. His motto is 'Let us eat and drink for tomorrow we die'. He observes, it is true, the old maxim of rising at an early hour in the morning, not however for the sake of enjoying the cool breeze, and taking moderate exercise, but rather to begin the day's career of eating

and drinking. His first essay is usually a *sopie* or glass of gin, to which succeed a cup of coffee and a pipe. His stomach thus fortified, he lounges about the great hall of the house or the veranda if in the country, with a loose night gown carelessly thrown over his shoulders, a night cap and slippers, till about eight o'clock, which is the usual hour for breakfast. This is generally a solid meal of dried meat, fish and poultry made into curries, eggs, rice, strong beer and spirits. Curry and rice is a standing dish at all meals and at all seasons of the year, being considered an excellent stimulus to the stomach. The business of the day occupies little more than a couple of hours, from ten to twelve, when he again sits down to dinner, a meal that is somewhat more solid than breakfast.

(JOHN BARROW, *A VOYAGE TO COCHINCHINA*, 1806)

By the middle of the eighteenth century, the Dutch East India Company claimed to exercise political control over most of Java. But this political control was tenuous and there was no accompanying impact in terms of Dutch culture or technology. There was, however, an economic impact, as the Dutch, working through the Javanese elite and Chinese tax agents, developed ways to raise money and extract the maximum agricultural production for the Company's benefit.

Yet it was not until the nineteenth century and subsequently in the twentieth century, that the Dutch presence began to have a major effect on the lives of most Indonesians. That effect came as the Dutch responded to the growing market for tropical goods in Europe and as they reacted to the activities of other foreign powers in the Southeast Asian region. From the Dutch point of view, these twin pressures of economic demand and foreign competition meant that it was no longer sufficient to maintain a loose control over the scattered islands, working from a limited number of bases in association with local rulers. Instead, the Dutch government in the Indies—for the Dutch East India Company had been abolished at the end of the eighteenth century—began to establish a closer control and more uniform administration in the areas it saw as vital to its interests. This policy sometimes led to sharp conflict with local forces, and in areas of Sumatra the Dutch had to fight for decades before they were able to achieve dominance at the end of the nineteenth century. Previewing the continuing sense of a separate and distinctive identity that is present in modern-day Aceh, this area of northern Sumatra posed the greatest resistance to the establishment of Dutch rule. And Bali, too, despite its modern image as a tourist-friendly society, was the scene of short but bitter resistance to the Dutch advance at the beginning of the twentieth century.

By the early twentieth century, the Dutch claimed control of all of the Archipelago stretching from Sumatra in the west to the western part of New Guinea in the east as the result of conquest and treaty. Only the tiny colony of Portuguese Timor escaped the Dutch net. The Dutch flag now flew over a strikingly diverse group of islands in which levels of development ranged from the distinctive and refined world of central Java to the modern stone age still found in New Guinea. Given this diversity, the impact of the alien Europeans also varied widely, ranging from increasing impoverishment of the peasantry in central and eastern Java to the implantation of Christianity in such sharply different regions as the Toba highlands in Sumatra and the outer Indonesian island of Ambon.

Of all the changes and developments that came with Dutch rule, none was more important than the sense that emerged among the colonised Indonesians that it was possible to think of common interests uniting all the peoples of the Archipelago. Here was the basis for a future sense of shared Indonesian national identity. In distant historical times there had been Javanese rulers who had thought in terms of a *Nusantara*, an 'empire of the islands'. As the result of foreign rule, the outlines of such an empire were established, and in a clearer and firmer fashion than had ever seemed possible before. The final creation of the Indonesian Republic was the work of Indonesians, but this work was carried out within a framework that in considerable part was laid down during the period of Dutch colonial rule.

Malaysia, Singapore and Brunei

Like Indonesia, modern Malaysia owes its existence and its geographical boundaries to the colonial period. In traditional times, the present state of Malaysia was part of a wider Indonesian-Malay world. Malay sultans ruled in states of varying size along the coasts of peninsular Malaysia, the northern regions of the great island of Borneo and in eastern Sumatra.

European expansion into this area was a slow and haphazard affair. The Portuguese capture of Malacca in 1511 was not followed by any major advance into the area of modern Malaysia until the final decades of the eighteenth century. By that time the Dutch had replaced the Portuguese in Malacca and the British had established a settlement on the island of Penang in 1786. Settlement of Singapore followed in 1819 and by the 1830s, the British had advanced to the point where they held three settlements on the fringe of the Malayan Peninsula—Singapore, Penang and Malacca. Known as the Straits Settlements, these three British possessions proved a magnet for Chinese immigrants, so that by the middle of the nineteenth century, Chinese were the largest ethnic group in the populations of each of them.

Immigrant Chinese were essential to the Straits Settlements, filling an extraordinary range of occupations. The following is a description from 1879 of the positions they filled.

The Chinese are everything; they are actors, acrobats, artists, musicians, chemists, druggists, clerks, cashiers, engineers, architects, surveyors, missionaries, priests, doctors, schoolmasters, lodging house keepers, butchers, porksellers, cultivators of pepper and gambier, cakesellers, cart and hackney carriage owners, cloth hawkers, distillers of spirits, eating house keepers, fishmongers, fruit-sellers, ferrymen, grass-sellers, hawkers, merchants and

agents, oil sellers, opium shopkeepers, pawnbrokers, pig dealers,
and poulterers. They are rice dealers, ship chandlers, shop-keepers,
general dealers, tobacconists, vegetable sellers, planters, market-
gardeners, labourers, bakers, millers, barbers, blacksmiths,
boatmen, bookbinders, boot and shoemakers, brickmakers,
carpenters, cabinet makers, carriage builders, cartwrights, cart and
hackney carriage drivers, charcoal burners and sellers, coffinmakers,
confectioners, contractors and builders, coopers, engine drivers,
and firemen, fishermen, goldsmiths, gunsmiths and locksmiths,
masons and bricklayers, mat, kajang and basket makers, oil
manufacturers, and miners . . .

(J.D. VAUGHAN, *THE MANNERS AND CUSTOMS OF THE CHINESE OF THE
STRAITS SETTLEMENTS*, 1879)

At first, relations between the Straits Settlements and the
Malay sultanates of the Peninsula were limited, but this situation
changed as these sultanates became bases for the traders,
merchants, tin miners and labourers who began to play an
important role in the exploitation of the region's tin mines. In a
reversal of the usual proposition, this was a case where the flag
followed trade, so that as commerce developed, Britain came first
to be the most powerful political player in the region and then to
build on that position to take direct political control of affairs.

By the time of the First World War, British control extended
over the whole of peninsular Malaya in addition to the Straits
Settlements. Together the two political conglomerates formed an
economic whole and a more or less unified political entity. But
whatever had been achieved in economic and political terms, the
result of colonial advance into the area of modern peninsular
Malaysia had not been the achievement of unity in terms of the
interests of the original Malay population. Chinese immigrants
predominated in the Straits Settlements, but in the Malay
sultanates of the Peninsula, the Malays retained special rights as
'the people of the country'. But they held these special rights
against a background of greater economic advance on the part of

two other communities, the European and the Chinese. As the result of colonialism, a plural society, divided along ethnic grounds, had come into being.

The importance of the European powers in the creation of new political boundaries is clearly apparent in relation to peninsular Malaysia but nothing could make the point more plainly than the developments that took place in Borneo, in the areas that have come to constitute East Malaysia (modern Sarawak and Sabah) and Brunei. While Brunei became a British protectorate in 1888, Sarawak and Sabah were brought under a measure of European political control by two of the most unusual colonial powers to operate in Southeast Asia.

In Sarawak, the agent of colonial advance was not a government but an individual, James Brooke, the first of the 'white rajahs' about whom so much has been written. In Sabah, by contrast, the colonial power was a commercial venture, the Chartered Company of North Borneo. Yet even in these two cases, the fundamental thread that has linked much of the commentary on developments in the maritime world was once again present. In Sabah and Sarawak, as elsewhere, the very existence of the later post-colonial states was the partial result of the European advance. Where no comparable state had existed before and no boundary lines had been drawn, the nineteenth century witnessed the establishment of new political entities.

The Philippines

Just as was the case with Indonesia and Malaysia, the Philippines gained its territorial boundaries as the result of Spanish colonial occupation. Before the arrival of the Spanish there was no state that could be described as the Philippines. And just as the Dutch moved slowly to establish their control over the many islands making up modern Indonesia, so did the Spanish only slowly extend their control over the Philippines. And not only slowly, for their control over the islands making up the Philippines was also incomplete. By the middle of the eighteenth century, Spain was able to dominate the lowland areas of the northern Philippines islands, but the highland regions remained outside their control. Moreover, the southern Muslim areas of the Philippines never came under real Spanish control. Repeated Spanish attempts to dominate the fiercely independent sultanates of the southern regions failed. Spanish control was achieved in some major ports, such as Zamboanga, and their immediate surroundings, but the Sultan of Sulu and his less-powerful compatriots never submitted to Spanish rule. The seeds of contemporary Muslim separatism in the southern Philippines were sown long ago.

While the Philippines' experience of European colonialism had similarities with what occurred in Indonesia and Malaysia, in terms of the establishment of a new state with fixed boundaries, an additional and distinctive element was involved. This was the role played by the Catholic church. Conversion to the religion of the invading colonial powers took place elsewhere, notably in Vietnam. But nowhere else in Southeast Asia—Portuguese Timor included, before 1975—did the religion of the colonisers become the majority religion of the colonised. Yet this was what happened in the northern and central islands of the Philippines, leading to the situation today in which Christianity is the religion of some 90 per cent of the Philippine population.

Working hand in hand, the Spanish administration and the Catholic church with its priests and friars developed a new framework for society. Building on the village structure of pre-colonial times, the Spaniards introduced a new, non-indigenous system which encouraged the development of large landed estates. Indigenous elements certainly survived under Spanish rule, but the administrative, economic and religious structures the colonising power introduced had a profound effect.

This eventually led to a major historical irony. Filipinos became dissatisfied with Spanish rule when it became clear that the colonial power would not allow *Indios*—the non-Spanish inhabitants of the islands—to enjoy the same civil and ecclesiastical rights as did the Spaniards themselves. Yet the *Indios* who claimed these rights were the products of Spanish schools, seminaries and universities. The Spaniards who ruled the Philippines created a situation that had no parallel elsewhere in Southeast Asia. Their colonial subjects began their revolt against Spanish rule in the nineteenth century because they were, in effect, excluded from being Spanish. In their resentment of the barriers placed in their way, the Filipinos established their own national identity, one that nonetheless remained inseparably linked with the experience of Spanish rule and the importance of Catholicism.

East Timor

Within nine years of their having captured the great trading city of Malacca in 1511, the Portuguese established a small settlement in eastern Timor, itself one of the most easterly islands of the Indonesian Archipelago. They were drawn to this remote spot by the abundant supply of sandalwood found there, and there, in a haphazard fashion, they remained until the 1970s. Until the nineteenth century, their impact on the local population was extremely limited. Even their very survival as essentially indolent colonists was threatened from time to time as the Dutch, who had a position in the west of the island, looked at the Portuguese settlement with avaricious eyes. Indeed, this petty rivalry was not finally resolved until treaties were concluded between Holland and Portugal, first in 1816 and finally in 1914. In comparison with the impact of European colonialism elsewhere in Southeast Asia, the Portuguese in East Timor had a remarkably limited effect, except for their overseeing the formation of a tiny, largely mixed-race, elite in the territory's capital, Dili.

The emphasis in this chapter on the administrative results of the European colonial advance highlights only one aspect of a complex process. Beyond these administrative matters, particularly those concerned with the establishment of colonial states and their borders, other developments were taking place which are examined in the chapters that follow. Colonial powers established the borders of states and played a part in shaping the character of their populations, but in the final analysis, indigenous Southeast Asians determined how they should live, and by what standards. This is a point to be remembered constantly when the challenge and the advance of the Europeans into Southeast Asia are considered and assessed.

5

Economic
transformation

Viewed from the perspective of the early 21st century, the colonial impact on the countries of Southeast Asia had some puzzling and even contradictory effects. Following the European advance into the region, Southeast Asians found they were controlled by alien newcomers who were strangers to their cultures and values. Over time, resentment of this situation led to the emergence of nationalist movements seeking independence. But this was not the only consequence of the colonial years; another, of the greatest importance, was the economic transformation of Southeast Asia.

Beginning slowly in the seventeenth century, the economic transformation involved the participation of the indigenous population. Yet the decisions that led to great economic changes were not taken by them but by the colonial powers which ruled over all but one of the countries in the region; the exception being Thailand. Many of the changes were unquestionably negative for the indigenous populations. This does not alter the fact that change of momentous proportions took place, particularly from the nineteenth century onwards.

Transforming the landscape

To fly above Southeast Asia on a clear day is to be struck by the great contrast between areas of land that have been brought into agricultural or mineral production and those which have not. Whether over the mainland or over the sea, the work of man is evident. Vast rice fields spread across river deltas. Open-cut mining leaves bleached scars on the ground below. The ordered patterns of rubber and oil palm plantations stand out from the chaotic world of the still-uncleared jungle. It is staggering to realise how much of this landscape did not exist one hundred years ago. Rubber plantations, to take the most obvious example, are essentially a development of the early years of the twentieth century. A relatively small number of plantations were planted in the late nineteenth century, but the great expansion of rubber-growing began after 1900 in response to the demands of the European and American capitalist worlds.

The expansion of rice-growing in Southeast Asia is another example of the tremendous changes that took place from the nineteenth century onwards, and owed much to the establishment of European colonial control. Transforming the Mekong River Delta in southern Vietnam from a maze of swamps and undirected watercourses had begun before the French arrived in the early 1860s. As change took place in the last two decades of the nineteenth century and the early decades of the twentieth, it was still Vietnamese who, often working under backbreaking conditions, contributed the labour, just as it was a few elite Vietnamese who reaped the benefits of the changes taking place. But the fact that such great changes took place depended on European colonial control, and on European capital which provided the finance that made draining the delta possible and profitable. Eventually, it was the fact that Europeans controlled Vietnam that led to deep resentment of this economic system. For the transformation of the Mekong Delta did not bring rich rewards to the many, but only to the few.

Exports and exploitation

To understand the importance of the economic changes that took place in the nineteenth and twentieth centuries, it is essential to recognise that colonial control introduced a *new* economic system to Southeast Asia. There was, of course, economic activity in the traditional Southeast Asian world. The great empire of Srivijaya was a forerunner of later maritime states that sought to gain wealth through monopoly of the sea routes and the markets. Even in such states as Angkor, where participation in external commerce was not a major part of national life, complex internal economic patterns existed to maintain and staff the many temples that formed such a vital feature of Cambodian life. But this was not an economic system that depended on capital and commerce. In contrast, Malacca, before it fell to the Portuguese in the early sixteenth century, was a flourishing international commercial entrepôt. Additionally, Chinese and Japanese junks traded into the 'southern seas'. Caravans of merchants travelled slowly across the heart of the mainland regions, and inter-island trade in the maritime world was as much part of life in pre-colonial times as it continued to be once the Europeans arrived.

The prospect of becoming involved in the existing pattern of trade and so of gaining wealth was one of the single most important factors in bringing the Europeans to Southeast Asia in the first place. They wanted to gain a part, the largest part, of an existing spice trade that promised vast riches. The Iberians—the Portuguese and the Spanish—wanted more. While they wanted converts to their Catholic religion, the possibility of winning souls for Christ never excluded the possibility of gaining wealth through trade. In the case of the Philippines, as it happened, there were great disappointments for the Spanish when it was found what little opportunity existed for the development of profitable exports from that country, at least in the early stages of Spanish rule.

For a period, in the sixteenth and seventeenth centuries, the Portuguese and then the Dutch succeeded in their aims. They gained a monopoly of the spice trade in Southeast Asia, more exactly in Indonesia, controlled the supply of these commodities for the European markets and so reaped vast profits. In doing so, they commenced a process of peasant impoverishment in the Indonesian world that has left its mark to the present day. The Dutch aimed at complete control of the spice trade and worked to achieve it through the destruction of spice trees outside selected areas. Beginning as aliens working within the existing system, the Dutch, through their technological and organisational superiority, then began to alter that system to their advantage. Whole islands that had once formed part of the traditional pattern of trade were suddenly removed from participation. Even where production was still permitted, trees were destroyed to meet short-term Dutch efforts to maintain high price levels. In this way, economic activity in Southeast Asia became closely linked to the European market economy as it had never been before.

As the Dutch succeeded in controlling the spice trade in cloves and nutmeg in the eastern parts of the Indonesian Archipelago, and pepper production in the western islands, so during the eighteenth century they went on to gain ever greater control over the production and marketing of agricultural crops in Java. The production of coffee, in particular, came under strict Dutch regulation. Working through local rulers and Chinese agents, the Dutch were at one remove from this process. But it was they who determined upon the system of 'forced deliveries', that required a set amount of the crop to be made available to the East India Company under threat of severe punishment of whole villages if the goods were not supplied by the farmers who lived in them. At the same time, the Dutch expectation was that the Indonesians who furnished the goods so much in demand in Europe would themselves provide a market for the manufactured goods, particularly textiles, that could be brought to Southeast Asia in Dutch ships.

It would be wrong to suggest that by the beginning of the nineteenth century the Indonesian islands that had become part of the Dutch colonial economic system were already facing the prospect of economic disaster. Nevertheless, by that time, a system had been established which put the interests of the colonial power, and its agents, above all else. This left the bulk of the population at a clear disadvantage. Such a pattern was to be reinforced as the economy of Indonesia, and the whole of Southeast Asia, became more diverse and more closely linked to a broad range of European interests in the nineteenth century.

For the nineteenth century was when Europe felt the full force of the Industrial Revolution. That technological revolution played a major part in accelerating the search for colonial possessions overseas. Colonies, viewed in their simplest form, were seen as essential parts in the economic pattern that required the supply of raw materials to the industrial countries of Europe. Once processed, these raw materials could be sold to the markets of the world, including, if possible, the colonies from which the materials originally came. In retrospect, of course, the whole system appears quite remarkably and unfairly balanced in Europe's favour. Southeast Asians were expected to play an uncomplaining part in a process that enriched their colonial masters but offered little reward to them or their fellows. This lack of balance did not trouble most of the Europeans concerned with the colonies. An essential feature of the expanding imperial age and the economic developments that went with it was a belief on the part of the Europeans involved that what they were doing was right, and just as importantly, necessary. Questions of equity or justice simply did not arise. The nineteenth-century colonisers saw the world in different terms, so that a Frenchman in the early 1860s could see nothing unrealistic or unreasonable in writing that 'nations without colonies are dead'. And he meant, of course, that these colonies would be controlled by Europeans who had the capacity to carry out a 'civilising mission', in the interest of their colonial subjects.

The belief that colonising powers had in some sense a duty to rule is summed up in Rudyard Kipling's poetic call to the Americans to 'take up the white man's burden'. The poem was written in 1899 at a time when there was debate in the United States about the desirability of assuming colonial control of the Philippines.

Take up the White Man's burden
Send forth the best ye breed,
Go bind your sons to exile
To serve your captives' need;
To wait in heavy harness
On fluttered folk and wild,
Your new caught sullen peoples,
Half devil and half child . . .

However unreasonable such thoughts may seem today, it would be wrong to ignore the strength of the feeling involved for men of that age. It was the feeling that drove men to develop rubber estates, to exploit mines, and to grow copra palms, often living in very difficult conditions in order to do so. Southeast Asia, like Africa, could supply many of the materials that became essential to the needs of modern Europe and America during the nineteenth and twentieth centuries. Tin from Malaya and Indonesia helped meet the industrial nations' demand for cheap tinplate for use in the bearings essential for fast-running factory machinery. Rubber from Indonesia, Malaya and French Indochina, helped meet the needs of societies that expected constant improvement in a range of items from motor car tyres to surgical equipment. Copra from coconut palms played a part in the vast expansion of the soap industry as rising living standards in Europe and America made personal cleanliness the norm rather than the exception.

Meeting the demand: major commodities

So, as Southeast Asia in the nineteenth century came to meet new demands from Europe, a new kind of relationship developed between the region and the industrial world. The old system, characterised by the Dutch-monopolised spice trade, faded in importance and a new pattern developed. It can best be understood in terms of the principal industries and commodities that were involved.

Rubber

The existence of natural rubber had been known for centuries before scientific advances in the nineteenth century led to the development of a stable substance, largely unaffected by temperature changes. Rubber was recognised as having a vast range of uses, but the problem remained of finding a reliable source of this commodity to replace the high-priced and erratic supply from South America.

Largely as the result of British enterprise in the last two decades of the nineteenth century, it was found that growing rubber in Southeast Asia was possible and potentially profitable. Although by this stage colonial expansion in the region was well-advanced, establishing rubber plantations became a further justification for colonial activity. For in one of the most notable links between supply and demand, the discovery that rubber could be grown profitably in Southeast Asia coincided with the sudden expansion of demand at the beginning of the twentieth century culminating in the period of the First World War.

Vast areas of the Malayan Peninsula, of Java and Sumatra, and of Vietnam and Cambodia were brought under rubber cultivation. Here was transformation indeed, for many of the areas that were planted with rubber had not been cultivated previously. Some statistics make the point. There were no rubber plantations in peninsular Malaya (modern West Malaysia) before the 1880s. Yet

A rubber plantation in Malaysia. The discovery that rubber could be grown profitably in much of Southeast Asia was a major factor in the modern economic transformation of the region. (PHOTOGRAPH COURTESY OF *FAR EASTERN ECONOMIC REVIEW*)

by the beginning of the 1970s, rubber plantations accounted for 65 per cent of all cultivated agricultural land, with one third of the agricultural work force engaged in the plantation industry. This is the most dramatic example of a pattern that existed throughout the region. Where once land was uncultivated, or covered in jungle, new plantations were established.

European managers were responsible for the establishment of rubber plantations and for their profitable operation. In the early years of a plantation's existence, life for these men was far from easy, a fact that is recorded in numerous first-hand accounts of a planter's life. Some planters' accounts are bitter; others, at least in retrospect, see the humour of their past experiences, as is the case with Leopold Ainsworth as he describes his first dinner after arriving at a plantation in northern Malaya in the years before the First World War. The first two courses had been disappointing, then came dessert.

> The last course consisted of banana fritters, which looked good and undoubtedly would have been but for the fact that the flavour of the bananas was lost in the overpowering taste of coconut oil in which they were fried. The meal terminated with coffee, which was equally shattering, though it was not until later that I discovered that its horrible flavour was due to the cook's invariable habit of using one of the manager's socks as a strainer. Nothing appeared to his mind more effective for the purpose as this, and he was modestly proud of his discovery, so that no amount of punishment or threats could wean him from the use of it, whilst confiscation of the offending article merely meant that ere long another would be stolen and conveniently hidden for secret use in the future.
>
> (LEOPOLD AINSWORTH, *THE CONFESSIONS OF A PLANTER IN MALAYA*, 1933)

Such vast enterprises required large investments of capital and this fact ensured that the ownership of large-scale rubber plantations was in the hands of foreigners or of that very small group within the indigenous communities who could provide the necessary capital and then wait five years for production to begin. So the benefits to Southeast Asians themselves were limited. Even in the field of labour, the employment opportunities in Malaya went to non-indigenous workers, as the plantation companies imported indentured labourers—labourers contracted to work for a set period and for a set wage—from India and Ceylon (Sri Lanka).

In Vietnam, the bulk of the labour force was Vietnamese, but the conditions under which they were recruited and worked were frequently scandalously exploitive.

Eventually, the inequities of the rubber economy were redressed to some extent by the growth of small holdings in the hands of the indigenous population, at least in Malaya and Indonesia, though never in the countries of French Indochina. And even then, putting rubber plantations in the hands of small holders was always opposed by the large plantation interests.

Tin

Tin-mining had been part of Southeast Asia's economic life for millennia before it assumed a sudden new importance in the nineteenth century with the growth of demand in Europe and America. Although deposits of tin are found elsewhere in the region, it was in Malaya (West Malaysia) that the industry developed to its greatest degree. There, from the 1870s onwards, the establishment of British political control over the Malay states enabled the rapid expansion of already-existing Chinese tin-mining enterprises. In the twentieth century, Chinese dominance in the industry was challenged by European capital and the greater technological efficiency of the extraction methods used by large Western firms. Although the Chinese share declined, this section of the industry, with its reliance on labour-intensive methods, was never overwhelmed by the capital-intensive Western firms which relied on the tin dredge for extraction of the metal.

Unlike the rubber-growing industry, competition for tin involved two different sets of non-indigenous groups, the Europeans and the immigrant Chinese. So, before the Second World War, Malaya's tin-mining industry was in the hands of two groups considered outsiders by the indigenous Malays, who regarded themselves as the only true owners of the land in the country known as British Malaya.

Rice

Rubber plantations were largely dependent on imported labour. The tin industry was in the hands of non-indigenous groups. But in the development of the most important Southeast Asian export crop of all, rice, the role of the indigenous peasant was vitally important.

Rice had been exported from Southeast Asia before the onset of a full-scale colonial advance in the mid-nineteenth century. But the volume of exports was small, and internal trade within a single country, from an area with a rice surplus to an area experiencing shortages, was more important than any export trade. Moreover, rice was not generally grown for export; the bulk of the rice produced before the nineteenth century was for subsistence, to feed the peasant farmers and their families.

An increasing world market in the second half of the nineteenth century stimulated a rapid expansion of the areas in Southeast Asia that could grow rice for export: the Mekong Delta in southern Vietnam; the Chao Phraya (Menam) River Delta in central Thailand; and the Irrawaddy River Delta in Burma. In Vietnam and Burma, the expansion of the rice-growing industry took place in a colonial context. In Thailand, by contrast, the almost equally rapid expansion occurred in an independent state.

The expansion of the main rice-growing areas of Southeast Asia quite literally changed the landscape. In the deltas of the Irrawaddy, the Chao Phraya and the Mekong, a bare 100 to 140 years ago, rice-growing took place on a sparse, scattered basis. Seen today, the deltas offer a vision of immense agricultural richness and are a testimony to the labours of the millions of anonymous peasants who drained the swamps, built the canals, and brought the rich soil into crop production. In the face of such evidence of agricultural richness, the question why these deltas, most particularly in Burma and Vietnam, became regions of major economic and social inequality demands an answer.

Put simply, the apparent promise of the open agricultural

frontier was never realised by the peasants of Burma and Vietnam because they were not equipped to supply more than their own labour. To grow rice was an age-old peasant activity and one that the peasants carried out with tireless efficiency. But in the developing conditions, more than labour was required. Above all, the financial demands of the expanding industry were beyond the peasant. Capital was required for seed, for equipment and to employ the labour necessary to ensure that the harvest was planted, irrigated, collected and shipped with the minimum of delay.

Almost from the beginning of the dramatic expansion of the rice-growing area in southern Vietnam, the peasants found that they had no role to play on the new large holdings except as tenants, at best, or more usually as labourers, at worst. Those who benefited from the expansion of Vietnam's rice-growing capacities and the expanding export trade were a relatively small number of rich Vietnamese landowners and the Chinese rice merchants and shippers of Cholon, Saigon's twin city. The landowners, with interests closely linked to the French colonial power, were able to raise capital and pay the labour necessary to bring new regions into production. The Chinese merchants and shippers who controlled the rice mills in Cholon provided an unsurpassed commercial network that no-one, Vietnamese or European, could challenge.

In Burma, the situation was a little more complicated and the eclipse of the peasant from other than a labouring role took a little longer. But the pattern was much the same. One point of difference resulted from Burma's administrative link with India. Administered as 'part' of British India until the 1930s, Burma was open to virtually unrestricted immigration from India and many of these immigrants were to play a major, and largely negative, social role in the development of the rice-growing industry of Lower Burma. The long-term trend was one in which Indians slowly drove out the Burmese from many of the essential sections of the rice industry, in part because Indians controlled the operation of rural credit in the Burmese countryside. Burmese landlords remained an important element in the overall scheme of things but, like the Vietnamese landowners who profited from the Mekong Delta rice fields, they were separated in almost every sense from their workers, except for their Burmese ethnic identity.

The history of the rice industry in Thailand was very different. It would be wrong to suggest that no peasants suffered as the result of the expansion of rice-growing in the Chao Phraya Delta region of Thailand. Yet if there were losers in this massive development, there were certainly far fewer than elsewhere and the social costs were notably smaller. Unlike what occurred in Burma and Vietnam, the exploitation of the previously untilled delta lands in Thailand was the essential prerogative of the peasant farmer. Just why this should have been so is not completely clear, but the main reasons are not hard to find. The fact that Thailand was not a colony of an external power was of cardinal importance. The Thai government was not responsible to some distant parliament, ministry or electorate that expected colonies to pay their way. Instead, the control of agricultural development was in the hands of the Thai monarch and his close advisers. It was they rather than foreign commercial interests who determined the broad pattern of developments, which saw the peasants retaining land ownership and the size of land holdings much more restricted than was the case in Burma and Vietnam. The availability of capital was important in Thailand, too. Once again, the role of Chinese rice millers and merchants was essential for expansion. Yet unlike the other two expanding areas linked to the export market, the relationship between peasants and merchants in Thailand could accurately be described as involving a sense of partnership rather than exploitation.

Other export commodities

Rubber, tin and rice were among the most important of the commodities exported from Southeast Asia. But there were many more that contributed to the character of the region's economy, in particular its dependence on capital investment and the use of wage labour. The development of copra plantations, for instance, followed the pattern set by the rubber industry, though on a much smaller scale. A range of other crops proved suitable for plantation development, including tobacco, coffee and, most importantly, sugar. This last crop developed as a major export item in Java and the Philippines. Drawing on the local population for its labour supply, the sugar industry played its part in shifting the balance of peasant labour away from subsistence farming to paid employment. The development of Southeast Asia's oil industry was less labour-intensive but required very substantial capital investment. As early as the 1880s, oil was being produced in Burma. Later, from the second decade of the twentieth century, oil production was an important export commodity from the Indonesian island of Sumatra and from the territories of Sarawak and Brunei in northern Borneo.

Social impact on the region

How widespread were the changes that have just been described? Should we imagine a situation in which, from the second half of the nineteenth century, Southeast Asia was 'gripped' by economic change so that no part of life was untouched by the expansion of export industries?

Clearly, this was not the case. In the more remote areas of the region, the inhabitants were at first largely, if not totally, unaware of the momentous changes that were occurring elsewhere. In many rural villages, life went on with only limited effects being felt from the establishment of plantations and mines and the expansion of rice-growing areas. Village cultural life demonstrated an extraordinary resilience to outside pressures, even when these were not far distant geographically. Yet increasingly it has become clear that economic transformation did reach down and affect a remarkably broad range of Southeast Asian life.

The development of an export-oriented economy posed an alternative to subsistence farming and introduced those who were prepared to engage in wage labour to the concept of a cash economy. For most of the rural population, this was a totally new element that replaced traditional barter arrangements. The development of a cash economy went hand in hand with the slow but steady growth of a demand for consumer goods on which to spend wages. And this pattern encouraged the spread of petty retail business, usually run by one or other of the major immigrant groups in Southeast Asia, the Chinese and the Indians.

Developments of this sort were most obviously associated with areas in which plantation industries had immediately observable results. But there were other less obvious effects as a result of the transformation of the economies of the Southeast Asian countries. In Java, the changes that affected that island's economy were accompanied by a growth in the size of the rural population. As a result, and instead of seeking to escape from the increasing difficulties of rural life by migration to urban centres, Javanese peasants methodically set to work to grow more and more on what was, proportionately, less and less space. This was a highly negative development as the already harsh conditions of normal existence became worse. The value of land increased, not to the benefit of the average peasant but rather to the advantage of the moderately well-to-do rural dweller. The downward cycle of rural poverty increased in pace.

Colonial officials were reluctant to publicise examples of rural discontent, so it is only through recent research that a better picture has been gained of the extent to which rapid economic change had widespread negative effects and sparked resentment in countries as different as Cambodia, Malaysia and Vietnam. In Cambodia, for instance, peasant discontent in the 1915–16 period led to protests involving no fewer than 100 000 rural dwellers. The new taxes the French colonial authorities had imposed, coupled with a requirement for unpaid labour, were deeply resented by the rural peasantry. Still living in a largely unchanged traditional world, they could see no benefit in the taxes and labour the French expected them to accept.

Change was widespread but uneven. There were not, as used to be suggested, two separate economies in the Southeast Asian countries—one linked to the world market and the other to a closed 'native' economy. Certainly, there were broad divisions within economic life, but these broad divisions were interrelated so that the life of a subsistence farmer as well as that of the wage labourer on a plantation were affected by the economic changes taking place.

Impact on cities and infrastructure

The development of cities provided one instance of the broad impact of general economic change. In the early nineteenth century, the number of cities of any size in Southeast Asia was very small. Royal capitals, such as Bangkok in Thailand, or Yogyakarta in central Java, had populations that were numbered in tens, not hundreds, of thousands. Even the older capitals, such as Batavia (Jakarta) and Manila, had populations of less than 200 000 after centuries of an alien presence. Saigon, in 1820, had a population of about 180 000, but was by far the largest urban settlement in Vietnam, a country that the French in the 1860s accurately described as being almost without cities.

The great cities of modern Southeast Asia date, for the most part, from the nineteenth century, at least in terms of having a metropolitan character with links to the wider world. Singapore provides the most dramatic example. When Thomas Stamford Raffles founded a British settlement there in 1819, Singapore was a tiny Malay fishing village with a population of less than two hundred permanent inhabitants. Its rapid growth in the nineteenth century was chiefly due to immigration from China in response

After becoming a British possession in 1819, Singapore grew rapidly in both size and importance. As Southeast Asia's principal entrepôt, its harbour was constantly filled with shipping, as seen in this early engraving c. 1840.

to a rapidly expanding economy. As *the* great entrepôt for the Southeast Asian region as a whole, Singapore's development was a vivid reflection of the economic changes that were taking place. After the opening of the Suez Canal in 1869, Singapore's role as a link between Asia and Europe was strengthened as the time required for a voyage to or from Europe was sharply reduced.

Just as the growth of cities was a feature of the nineteenth century, so too was the expansion of the infrastructure—of roads, canals and other forms of communication so essential to modern economic life. The effect of the new road and rail systems introduced in the nineteenth and twentieth centuries varied greatly from country to country, and often had effects that were not originally planned. The case of Malaya makes this point.

Until the end of the nineteenth century, almost all travel in Malaya was by water. Instead of the modern road and rail systems that carry traffic north and south, particularly on the west coast of the Peninsula, transport moved slowly across the sea and in an even more restricted fashion along the rivers that ran down from the central mountain range to the coast. The construction of a road and rail network took place to carry the growing quantities of tin and rubber that were produced as economic transformation played its part in this region. At first the population at large derived little benefit from these new communications systems, for they were designed to serve particular and mostly foreign commercial interests. Yet with the passage of time, the expanding communications systems came to be important for the Malay peasantry as well and to serve their interests. Settlement patterns in many parts of Southeast Asia changed to take account of the new infrastructure that developed during the nineteenth and twentieth centuries and which made ease of movement an expectation for large numbers of the population. Comfort may not be the most striking feature of travel by local bus or third-class train in the region, but no-one who has used such transport in modern Southeast Asia can doubt the importance and relative ease of travel that has become such an accepted feature of daily life.

From the middle of the nineteenth century onwards, the broad lines of economic development are clear, as is the importance of those developments. Southeast Asia, in a period of less than one hundred years, changed from being a region in which exports played a relatively minor role and subsistence farming was essentially dominant, and became a vital area in the world economy. Its exports met European and American demands that had been fuelled by the great changes that had followed the industrial revolution. As Southeast Asia's export economy developed, more general economic and social change penetrated almost every level of society, leaving only the most isolated regions and populations untouched. The growth of great metropolitan cities, the rise of exports and the development of a cash economy, the institution of new communications systems, and the introduction of modern banking—all these were products of economic change in a period beginning a bare 150 years ago. Between the mid-nineteenth century and the outbreak of the Second World War, Southeast Asia's economy underwent greater change than at any other time in the region's entire history.

6

The Asian immigrants

Since the middle of the nineteenth century, Southeast Asia's cities have proved a magnet for migrants, a development that is closely associated with the dramatic economic changes that took place in the region after that time. A large proportion of migrants came from China and the Indian subcontinent, including Sri Lanka. Not only the cities experienced an influx of migrants; many Chinese immigrants initially engaged in agriculture, and immigrant labour from India and Sri Lanka was the mainstay of the plantation industry in Malaya. The presence of immigrant communities is abundantly apparent in Singapore and Malaysia, not so much by clothing nowadays, as was the case until quite recently, as by appearance. The descendants of dark-skinned Tamils from southern India and Sri Lanka contrast with the Chinese, and indeed, with the immigrants from northern India. But if Singapore and the cities of Malaysia offer an immediate sense of the importance of past immigration, immigrant communities can also be found in other Southeast Asian cities, even if not on the same scale. Bangkok has a quarter seldom visited by tourists that seems to belong to the sub-continent, and features sari shops, curry houses and Indian-language newspapers. Perhaps rather more surprising is the fact that the northern Thai city of Chiang Mai has a long-established community of Muslims whose original homes were in what today are India and Pakistan. Less readily identifiable, in terms of appearance, is the role that has been played by the descendants of Arabs from the Middle East in both Malaysia and Indonesia.

Technically, the term 'immigrant' applies only to the first generation of settlers who left their homes to come and live in a foreign country. But in Southeast Asia, the term has an extended meaning, applying to the groups of settlers who established new communities that were, for generations, regarded as living *in* but not *belonging* to the country in which they lived. The case of colonial Malaya makes this differentiation clear. Before the Second World War, and despite their great importance for the economy of the country, most of the many Chinese living in Malaya were not regarded as permanent settlers. This fact is less surprising when it is realised that the majority of the Chinese population at this time had not been born in Malaya. Moreover, where members of the immigrant Chinese community had political interests, these were linked to their homeland, where communists and nationalists were at war with each other and with the invading Japanese. Very much the same was true of the members of the ethnic Indian community in Malaya at the same time. The majority had been born in India and that was where they directed their political interests, in their case, in support of the anti-colonial movement against British rule in their homeland.

Immigration before the nineteenth century

Immigration in its various forms is as old as Southeast Asia's history. In prehistoric times, waves of immigrants moved south through

Three faces of an immigrant society—Malays, Chinese and Indians in Singapore.

Singapore provided the most dramatic examples of an immigrant society in Southeast Asia. Sparsely settled by less than two hundred Malays when Raffles took possession of Singapore for Britain in 1819, it is today a thriving state of more than 3.8 million. Chinese compose 77 per cent of the population, Malays 15 per cent, Indians 6 per cent and other races the balance of 2 per cent.

In these photographs dating from the late 1970s, Malays are seen returning from Friday prayers, Chinese watch traditional theatre, and Indians stand by their doorway in the predominantly Indian Serangoon Road area.

mainland Southeast Asia. In the maritime region, too, there were broad movements of populations in prehistoric times. Specialists still argue about the nature and direction of these movements. A measure of their significance and scale is the fact that outposts of Indonesian culture may be found in as distant a location as the island of Madagascar lying off the east cost of Africa.

As prehistory blends into history, there is evidence of another form of migration—a very limited and selective population movement rather than the large-scale changes that apparently took place several thousand years ago. This was the migration of priests and traders discussed in Chapter 1. In general, large-scale migration was not part of Southeast Asia's classical period. What took place was the arrival of a relatively limited number of men—for few women were involved—from India and then, rather later, from China. Chou Ta-kuan, in his account of Angkor in the thirteenth century, refers to his Chinese countrymen living in the great Cambodian city. They were mostly sailors who had settled in Cambodia and become traders, marrying local women and with their descendants becoming absorbed within the local population in a generation or two.

The advance of ethnic Thai into the territories of modern Thailand was a major example of migration that took place in the latter part of the classical period and in succeeding centuries. Just what was involved here is another subject of controversy. Was there a mass movement of an ethnic group, or did an elite group of immigrants succeed in imposing their language and culture on an existing population? The balance of opinion seems to be shifting towards substantial population movement, but if this is correct, what happened in Thailand contrasts with the rest of Southeast Asia.

Leaving aside the forced movement of large numbers of people from one area to another as prisoners of war and the example of Thailand just noted, mainland Southeast Asia by the end of the classical period was not an area in which major migrations occurred. Vietnam, once again, was an exception. From the achievement of independence from China in 939 CE, the Vietnamese population slowly but surely moved southwards into territories that had been controlled by Champa and Cambodia. This *nam-tien* (southern march, or advance) was still in progress when the French colonialists arrived in the nineteenth century.

For the rest of Southeast Asia, in both the mainland and maritime regions, what had begun to develop very slowly was what Chou Ta-kuan had observed at Angkor: individuals and families came in small numbers to Southeast Asia in response to the opportunities they saw in foreign lands. Some of these immigrants were quickly absorbed into the existing population. Others, such as the communities of traders associated with the great port city of Malacca, maintained their sharply different ethnic identities. At the height of Malacca's power and fame in the fifteenth and early sixteenth centuries, the great port city had major communities of Arabs and Chinese, Indians from different regions, Indonesians from many islands, and Persians, to mention only the most prominent members of the cosmopolitan population. Almost certainly, these people, living far from their place of birth, did not think of Malacca as their home. They might die or have children in Malacca, but their home remained in a distant region across the sea.

Until very recently, this continued to be the attitude of the great majority of non-indigenous communities living in Southeast Asia. Individual immigrants might become important within a particular state so that their descendants blended completely into what had once been an alien culture for their ancestor. The Thai kingdom provides just such a case in which a Persian family settled in Ayuthia in the seventeenth century and rose by the nineteenth century to be among the most powerful in the land. Today, descendants of this family, the Bunnags, are still prominent in many fields of Thai public life.

The Baba Chinese were one group that did not conform to the general pattern that existed before the nineteenth century. These were descendants of immigrants from China who had settled in Malacca and lived in a world that was half-Chinese and half-Malay, never completely one nor the other. But perhaps their most distinctive characteristic was that they *did* regard themselves as permanent settlers in Malaya. And in a somewhat similar fashion, the Chinese *mestizo* community in the Philippines, most notably in Manila, were a group that sank deep roots into what had originally been an alien land. This mestizo community was already important by the eighteenth century and the descendants of the mixed alliances between Chinese and Filipinos played a vital role in Philippine life that continues to the present day.

Until the nineteenth century, the immigrant communities in Southeast Asia were small. Even in Batavia (Jakarta), the largest colonial city of the the time, the number of Chinese at the end of the eighteenth century was only a little more than 20 000. Members of these immigrant communities engaged in commerce that was, for the most part, shunned by Southeast Asians themselves. In the territories controlled by the Dutch and Spanish the indigenous populations regarded them not only as temporary inhabitants but also as having with their interests firmly linked to the colonial powers.

Signifcant changes in the nineteenth century

When change came in the nintennth century, nowhere was the impact of Asian immigration more obvious than in the British colonial possessions that came to be known as the Straits Settlements (Penang, Malacca and Singapore) and Malaya. Of these, Singapore provides the most dramatic example of how Asian immigration into Southeast Asia transformed the previously existing political and ethnic balance.

Singapore

When Thomas Stamford Raffles took possession of Singapore for the British Crown in 1819, his actions 'removed' a haunt of fishermen and pirates from the surrounding Malay world. Raffles' aim to make Singapore the centre for international trade in Southeast Asia had an immediate effect. Manpower was needed to turn Singapore into an entrepôt and the hundred to two hundred Malay fishermen on the island could not provide this, even if they had wanted to.

Writing in 1864, John Cameron, a resident of Singapore, described the impact of the Chinese immigrants in the Straits Settlements:

> I now pass on to the Chinese population, which, though entirely the result of immigration since the British settlement in the Straits [Settlements], stands next to the Malays in the census of the colony—numbering over 120,000—at the three stations. They are by far the most industrious, and, consequently, the most valuable we have in these possessions—the development of which is almost entirely due to them . . . they are ambitious to become rich; and though this ambition had generally its origin in the desire to return to China in affluent circumstances, yet our possessions not the less benefit by their labour . . .

> (JOHN CAMERON, *OUR TROPICAL POSSESSIONS IN MALAYAN INDIA*, 1864)

Chinese immigrants, and, to a lesser extent, immigrants from India, were ready to supply the labour that Singapore required. The census figures tell the story. Within five years of Singapore's foundation, its population already totalled 10 000. Malay numbers had increased sharply to more than 4500, but the trend for the future was already clear. By the end of 1824, Singapore's Chinese population already numbered nearly 3500 where previously there had been no Chinese living on the island at all. Within twenty-five years of Singapore's foundation, the Chinese in the British colony were an absolute majority of the total population. Of the 52 000 residents in the mid-1840s, no less than 32 000, or 61 per cent, were Chinese and in a very real sense the colony was dependent on this immigrant community's labour and services. Scarcely a trade existed that was not filled by newcomers from China. As the years passed, a growing number of Chinese immigrants became men of substance, as wealthy and even wealthier than those European businessmen who had found excellent prospects in Singapore.

Malaya

Through being a barely inhabited island, Singapore was a special case in the Southeast Asian region as a whole. Nowhere else in the region experienced the same combination of commercial success and Chinese immigration that eventually formed the basis of a new state in which the descendants of immigrant Chinese were and are the dominant ethnic group. Yet this fact should not hide the importance of Chinese immigration elsewhere. Immigrant Chinese played an important economic role throughout Southeast Asia. This was particularly the case in Malaya during British colonial times, where the growth of a large Chinese community eventually posed political problems that remain to the present day.

When Britain started to extend its political control over the sultanates of the Malayan Peninsula from the mid-1870s onwards, there were already many thousands of Chinese working in the tin mines that had been developed from the middle of the century. As colonial law and order was imposed, there was an influx of Chinese labourers and merchants. The towns that grew up on the west coast of the Peninsula were overwhelmingly Chinese in character. Ipoh, Kuala Lumpur, Seremban and dozens of other smaller settlements were centres for Chinese commerce both large and small. Yet these Chinese men—for there were few women among the immigrants—did not see themselves as permanent residents of Malaya. For them, China was their homeland to which, if all went well, they would eventually return. This outlook, and the policy, or lack of it, of the British colonial authorities, meant that little or no thought was given to what would happen if the immigrants' dream of returning to China could not be satisfied.

Malaysia's modern capital, Kuala Lumpur, was a rough and ready mining settlement when Frank Swettenham, later a famous

British colonial administrator, visited it in 1872 in company with a lawyer, J. G. Davidson. He had come by steamer from Singapore to Klang on the coast, where arrangements were made to travel about 30 kilometres upriver to Kuala Lumpur.

> . . . The journey took three days, rowing and poling, and we were welcomed by the doughty Capitan China [Chinese headman] Yap Ah Loi . . .
>
> With the exception of the Capitan China's own house—which was more pretentious and more solidly built—the place consisted of thatched hovels with earthy flooring, some of them unoccupied. The next day while Davidson was making his enquiries, I wandered around Kuala Lumpur and went into what appeared to be an empty hut: it was quite empty, except for a dead Chinese, with a bullet hole in his chest, who was sitting on the red earth floor with his back against the wall.
>
> (FRANK SWETTENHAM, *FOOTPRINTS IN MALAYA*, 1942)

The Second World War changed this situation irrevocably. Returning to China ceased to be option. Then, when the war ended, the great political changes in China that accompanied the communist victory in 1949 meant that the old relationship between the communities of ethnic Chinese overseas and the Chinese state could never be the same again. But by the time the Second World War interrupted the apparent colonial calm of Southeast Asia the Chinese population resident in Malaya had grown to be nearly 40 per cent of the country's total population, a formidably large proportion and one that was increasingly seen as a threat by the growing numbers of politically conscious Malays.

Why did the Chinese immigrants succeed in Southeast Asia?

Why were Chinese immigrants so important in Singapore and Malaya and, though on a smaller scale, in so many other areas of

Southeast Asia? And how does one explain their commercial success?

There is a temptation to find answers to these questions in broad generalisations about Chinese 'commercial skill', or the ability of Chinese to succeed in business by really trying. The attraction of such answers is obvious—general answers to big questions without too much complicated analysis. In the end, such responses are unsatisfactory. This point is made clear by noting one fact that is often forgotten. A large proportion of Chinese immigrants into Southeast Asia came, worked, and died as coolies—labourers, working for low wages and doing hard, physically demanding work. The success of the Chinese immigrants who were businessmen should not obscure the existence of the poorly paid and often ill-treated labourers. Other Chinese immigrants worked in occupations far removed from the upper ranks of the commercial world, as market gardeners or as kitchen hands, as carpenters or as clerks. Success in business and access to great wealth was not a universal feature of life for the Chinese immigrant in Southeast Asia.

For those who were successful, some straightforward explanations are possible. Chinese immigrants in Southeast Asia often filled roles in society that others would not or could not fill. What happened in Vietnam after the French seized control of Saigon in 1861 makes the point. Finding the lack of a Vietnamese commercial class, the French encouraged Chinese to come to the city because they knew that Chinese businessmen could play a role for which no-one else in the colony—French or Vietnamese—was equipped. What was true in Vietnam was true elsewhere. Chinese immigrants were ready and able to undertake tasks that Southeast Asians themselves either shunned or for which they lacked training and expertise.

The role of a rural shopkeeper is a good example of the kind of position that a Chinese immigrant occupied. Southeast Asians, with some notable exceptions, did not regard commerce as an attractive way of life. Moreover, to engage in the business of small-scale shopkeeping in a rural area required capital and an understanding of a cash economy. Chinese immigrants had advantages here. Even if a man of ability did not have capital of his own, he could often gain access to funds through family or clan connections. And once he possessed funds, his knowledge of the workings of a cash economy enabled him to become not simply a vendor of goods but, in addition, to engage in a broader range of business, selling on credit to peasant farmers in return for a share of their crop, and lending money. It's easy enough to see why Chinese immigrants were often resented. A successful shopkeeper with interests extending into the rice industry and involved in money-lending could become a vital and sometimes oppressive figure on the rural scene.

Resentment of Chinese immigrants was also sometimes felt because of their links with colonial governments. As the presence of colonial governments became more and more a matter of resentment among the peoples of Southeast Asia, so did that resentment come to encompass those Chinese immigrants whose livelihood was linked with the alien, European authorities. In Indonesia, for instance, there was bitter resentment of the Chinese who acted as tax collectors and agents for the colonial government's opium monopoly.

Pathways and barriers to Chinese assimilation

Feelings against the Chinese immigrant communities in Southeast Asia were most acute in regions where a variety of social and religious factors made the prospect of assimilating the immigrants into the existing indigenous community extremely difficult, if not impossible. Only in Cambodia, Thailand and the Philippines has there been major assimilation of Chinese into existing societies. Elsewhere, with Vietnam as a partial exception, assimilation has been limited, even rare. In Indonesia and Malaysia, countries where Islam is the dominant religion, the reluctance of Chinese immigrants to embrace Islam has been a major barrier to assimilation. In Cambodia and Thailand, by contrast, the national religion of Buddhism provided a flexible framework within which immigrant Chinese found it possible to begin the assimilation process that was then carried on by later generations. The Catholic church in the Philippines may not, perhaps, be described as flexible in the same way as the Buddhist church in Thailand or Cambodia. However, it did not have Islam's dietary restrictions and possessed, in practice if not always in strict theory, considerable tolerance towards widely varying degrees of religious observance, and so Catholicism in the Philippines played a vital role in the process of assimilation.

In Cambodia and Thailand, it is still possible to see the process of assimilation of Chinese immigrants in action, particularly in rural towns where a family shophouse is occupied by several generations of the one family. The more recent generations, through inter-marriage and the adoption of local speech and customs, steadily leave behind the original ethnic identification of their forebears. The clues to this process may be seen in the mixing of local Buddha images with strips of red paper bearing gold Chinese characters offering the traditional wishes for health, wealth, long life and many descendants.

Whether welcomed or resented, assimilated or kept as a rigidly separated community, Chinese immigrants into Southeast Asia have played a major role in the region's history. Their economic role was most obvious, but time and again that economic role had important political implications. Above all, the presence of large numbers of unassimilated Chinese in these immigrant communities was transformed into a major political problem after the Second World War—the establishment of the Chinese People's Republic in 1949 meant that a return to their homeland was for most a personal and political impossibility.

Non-Chinese immigrant communities

While Chinese made up the largest of the immigrant communities in Southeast Asia, they were by no means the only group to seek a better way of life in the region. Some of the other immigrant communities were of minor importance for the broad history of the region, however important individual members might have been. The scattered immigrant communities from the Middle East are a case in point. Other immigrant communities were important in particular areas but not in others. In Cambodia and Laos, for example, the French encouraged Vietnamese migration since Vietnamese were ready to undertake the clerical duties required by the French colonial administration and engage in small-scale commerce that only rarely attracted Cambodian and Lao interest. Of all the other immigrant communities, only one other ethnic group played a part in economic life that even approached that played by the Chinese. This was the overseas Indian community.

Although we are aware of Indian immigration in Southeast Asia dating back to the earliest period of written records, major Indian immigration into the region did not begin until the nineteenth century. Like the Chinese, Indians came to Southeast Asia to fill positions that could not or would not be filled by Southeast Asians themselves. And like the Chinese, the bulk of the Indians who came to Southeast Asia did so because the chances for employment appeared better than in their native land.

Indian immigrants established themselves throughout Southeast Asia, but their numbers were greatest in Burma and the Malaya–Singapore region—for obvious reasons. India was administered by the British and as a result immigration from India was mostly to other British colonial possessions. Most of the Indians who emigrated were labourers, particularly plantation workers. But Indian labour became important in other spheres— in road-building and in railway work. The importance of Indian labour in these areas of activity may still be seen today by visitors to Malaysia.

Like the Chinese, again, Indian immigrants into Southeast Asia worked in a wide range of occupations. Some, such as members of the Sikh community, were recruited from India to occupy military and police positions that their caste or religious group had traditionally occupied in India. Others, among them money lenders, notably Chettyars—a South Indian caste—came of their own accord to practise a profession that frequently led to resentment: this arose when local Southeast Asian peasants found themselves deeply in debt to an alien. The activities of Indian money lenders in Burma were a major reason for the resentment felt by the Burmese towards Indians, a resentment that led, after Burma's independence, to a mass expulsion of Indians from the country.

Like other immigrants into Southeast Asia in the expanding economic opportunities of the nineteenth and early twentieth centuries, some who came from India prospered mightily. Indian immigrants and their first-generation descendants became successful businessmen, lawyers and doctors. Yet it is clear that a smaller proportion of Indian immigrants rose to the towering heights of commercial success achieved by some Chinese. There is debate about why this should have been so, but in general it seems a reflection of an unreadiness of most, if not all, Indian immigrants to become engaged in business ventures involving joint stock operations. Indian commercial success in Southeast Asia appears to have been very much at the family level and was never so far-reaching as for the Chinese.

A story of success—and tragedy

Asian immigration into Southeast Asia was one of the most important features of the great economic changes that took place from the middle of the nineteenth century. Immigrants provided the physical muscle, the energy, and later, the finance for much of the development that took place as Southeast Asia moved firmly, if unevenly, away from its traditional past. In Singapore, where the state that ultimately emerged at independence in 1963 was dominated by ethnic Chinese, and in Malaysia, where the Peninsula of Malaya came to have a population that was more than one third ethnic Chinese, the arrival and settlement of Chinese was, and is, of vital importance. Indian immigration into Malaya and Singapore was less numerous and correspondingly less significant, but vital nonetheless, as was Indian immigration into Burma.

The importance of these immigrant arrivals in Southeast Asia cannot disguise the resentment their presence caused. Initially, they filled jobs that Southeast Asians shunned or lacked the skills to carry out. But times changed and Southeast Asians came to resent the difficulty in gaining access to jobs held by immigrants or their descendants. At the same time, and as part of the long and turbulent process leading up to independence, Southeast Asians often came to identify immigrants with the colonial regimes ruling over them. Indians in Burma and Chinese in Indonesia were seen in this light.

Overall, it is difficult to write about the Asian immigrants who came to Southeast Asia without introducing a note of tragedy. For despite the many who prospered, and continue to do so, and despite the very special experience of Singapore, Asian immigration has always had an element of tragedy associated with it. For the early immigrants in the nineteenth century, it was the tragedy that would overtake them if they died in a foreign land. For later immigrants and their descendants, there was the special and very personal tragedy of finding they 'belonged' neither in the land of their ancestors nor, in the eyes of Southeast Asians, in the new land in which they had been born. On occasion, a sense of tragedy became powerfully apparent in the forced deportation of Indians from Burma or the large-scale killing of Chinese in the 1960s in Indonesia, when to be Chinese was to be regarded as a communist.

Asian immigrants were vital for the economic transformation of Southeast Asia, but for the most part, with Singapore as the exception, they were not to be among the political masters of the countries in which they lived when these eventually emerged into independence.

7

The years of illusion: Between the wars, 1918–41

If there is a popular memory of Southeast Asia while the colonial powers still held power, it surely relates to the years between the two world wars. This was the time that has been celebrated or mocked in films and novels with their settings in 'British Malaya', 'French Indochina' or the 'Netherlands Indies'. So, to an extent, the image of the European planter or official, his white tropical suit spotless or shabby according to his personal character, has become more than a figure in a Somerset Maugham story but rather a figure representative of an age. In the same way, the 1920s and 1930s have often, in popular memory, been seen as a period when Southeast Asians, 'natives' in the words used at the time, filled roles as patient and industrious peasants, faithful servants, courtly but ineffective princes and, rarely, as heroic rebels against colonial rule.

Yet the deeper we look below the surface of these images, the more it becomes clear that these generalisations of popular literature and travellers' tales hide a much more complicated past. The 1920s and the 1930s were, indeed, the time when colonial control of the countries of Southeast Asia was at its fullest extent, but it was also the period when the foundations of foreign rule in the region came under considerable strain. It was a period when modern nationalist movements became important. And, not least, it was a time when there were major revolts against foreign rule. Even now, it is difficult to be sure how many colonialists recognised this fact at the time.

Settled colonial boundaries and economic boom times

By the end of the second decade of the twentieth century, Southeast Asia possessed a pattern of boundaries that has changed little, right up to the present day. On the mainland there was a British colonial government in Burma; France ruled over Vietnam, Cambodia and the Lao states, with these three colonial possessions known as French Indochina. Thailand, alone, preserved its independence.

In the maritime world, the Dutch ruled the territories that were to become Indonesia, and America was the colonial power in the Philippines. In East Timor, the Portuguese maintained a tiny colonial presence. The situation was more complicated in relation to the territories that now form Malaysia and Singapore. Britain ruled over the Malayan Peninsula and Singapore, but in Sarawak, the Brooke family still held power, while a chartered company—a commercial operation that acted as a government— ruled the region that is now known as Sabah. Even if Sarawak and Sabah were administrative oddities, their links to Britain were clear. The eventual foundation of Malaysia between 1956 and 1963 was another example of a modern state inheriting the boundaries laid down during the period of colonial rule.

A French colonial official surrounded by his Lao assistants in 1930. (PHOTOGRAPH COURTESY OF GRANT EVANS)

With stable borders and the end of the First World War in 1918, the European powers that controlled the colonised states of Southeast Asia looked forward to a period of political calm and economic expansion. As far as the second of these hopes was concerned, the experience of the early 1920s seemed to match and even exceed their expectations. The economic expansion of Southeast Asia in the closing decades of the nineteenth century had transformed the region and left it ready to meet the demands of the peace-time boom that followed the war. With Southeast Asia as a prime source of rubber, rice and tin, the export earnings of the companies controlling the plantations, mines and paddy fields rose rapidly. Southeast Asian rubber made the tyres for the motor cars on which the Western world had come to depend.

Southeast Asian tin was in demand: for the manufacture of tinplate, reflecting the increased use of canned food, and as an essential element in the manufacture of specialised industrial equipment. And the rice grown in Southeast Asia fed populations from India to Europe.

The rise of nationalism and the role of communism

To the extent that they thought about the matter, colonial officials believed that this period of economic expansion would ensure that the colonised peoples would be ready to accept their lot, to be content with a situation in which all major decisions affecting their lives were taken by foreigners. Initially, this expectation seemed justified. In the early 1920s, calm seemed to be the general, though not absolutely complete, order of the day. Whether this was, in fact, due to the good economic times, is debatable. Just as important was the fact that it was not until the mid-1920s that modern political movements began to develop in Southeast Asia— movements that looked beyond the basic goal of independence and towards new ideas of how an independent state should be governed.

This development was what made the 1920s so important. Colonial governments had encountered resistance to their rule before. The Dutch had fought bitter colonial wars as they expanded their hold over the Indonesian islands in the nineteenth century, particularly in the Aceh region of northern Sumatra. In Burma, it took years of what the British called 'pacification', which was in effect a small-scale colonial war before peace was established throughout that country's territory, while in Vietnam, resistance to the French was almost continuous. Nevertheless, all of the movements that had resisted foreign rule in Southeast Asia before the First World War had been *essentially* traditional in character.

The change from traditional resistance to modern anti-colonial movements has usually been described as the growth of nationalism. But what does this description mean? To begin with, the 'growth of nationalism' involved the emergence of political movements after the First World War that were significantly different from the anti-colonial movements that existed in the nineteenth century. Developments in Indonesia make this very clear. The men who called for independence in the 1920s were very much aware of the past efforts of the men and women who had fought against the Dutch in such campaigns as the Java War (1825–30), the Paderi Wars in Sumatra (1820s and 1830s), and the Aceh War, again in Sumatra (1872–1908). But for a man such as Sukarno, who was to become the first President of Indonesia, getting rid of the Dutch was only one part of his political program. He and the other leaders of his generation wanted both the end to Dutch rule and the establishment of a new Indonesian *nation* where none had existed before. And this nation was to be governed according to a new set of political and social values, some linked to Indonesia's past and some adopted from Europe.

So, in Indonesia and elsewhere in Southeast Asia, this nationalism combined old and new, something of the values of the West as well as the values of Southeast Asia itself. Not surprisingly, given their values at this time, the colonial powers opposed these demands for basic change to the political control of territories they saw both as a source of wealth and of prestige. And given the imbalance between the power of the colonialists and the power of those they ruled, it seems surprising that the nationalists continued to have faith they could achieve their goal of independence. At the very least, the odds seemed stacked against the nationalists who were seeking independence. As they pursued their goals of independence, the nationalists encountered implacable opposition from the colonial powers, which were ready to impose their will and maintain control through drastic means.

If we try to answer the question of why a new, modern nationalism came into being in the 1920s, an important part of the explanation involves *awareness*. Partly as a result of the time that had passed since the colonial powers established themselves in the countries of Southeast Asia, and partly in response to developments in other parts of the world, the early leaders of the modern nationalist movements in countries such as Vietnam and Indonesia became aware that there were alternatives to their colonial status. With the spread, even though it was on a limited basis, of Western-style education in the colonies of Southeast Asia, young men and women became aware of the revolutions that had taken place in Europe and America, as well as in China. They began to ask why they, too, could not change a system which left foreigners in charge of their countries' destinies. And they became aware of Western political ideas that supported their desire for independence.

Mohammad Hatta, one of the most important Indonesian nationalists, was an example of a man whose exposure to Western education helped shape his determination to work for an independent Indonesia. An outstanding student, Hatta was sent by the Dutch to study in Holland, where he spent nearly ten years studying economics. He found the contrast between the liberal atmosphere of Holland and the restrictions placed on his compatriots in Indonesia by the colonial regime both striking and disturbing. Convinced that change had to take place and that Indonesia had a right to be independent, he vigorously argued this point of view when he returned from Holland in 1932. As a result, he was imprisoned by the Dutch as a troublemaker and was not released until the Japanese army overran the Netherlands Indies in the Second World War.

Ho Chi Minh of Vietnam, probably the best-known of all those who sought independence from a colonial power through revolution, gained his knowledge of the West and its political theories in a very different fashion from the way Hatta did. Unlike Hatta, Ho was never seen as a model student. Instead the French administration in Vietnam saw him as the troublesome son of a minor official who refused to cooperate with the colonial government. Ho left Vietnam at an early age to work as a member of a ship's crew and found his way to Europe and to a series of low-paid jobs in London and Paris. It was in Paris that he became acquainted with the revolutionary writings of Karl Marx and Lenin and with their call for a world-wide revolution of the working classes. Convinced that communism offered the answer to the major political problems of the world, including colonialism, Ho became one of the founder member of the French Communist Party. This fateful step was to lead him along an extraordinary path of personal hardship, imprisonment and eventual triumph in his battle to end French rule over Vietnam.

Ho Chi Minh was one of the most remarkable of the Southeast Asian revolutionaries who challenged colonial rule. Living as an exile from Vietnam for thirty years of his life, he embraced communism in the belief that it would provide the revolutionary philosophy that would drive the French from his country.
(PHOTOGRAPH COURTESY OF *FAR EASTERN ECONOMIC REVIEW*)

Still using the name Nguyen Ai Quoc (Nguyen who loves his country), and before the Vietnamese Communist Party was founded at the beginning of the 1930s, Ho Chi Minh had already embraced communism as the answer to Vietnam's colonial situation. Writing in 1927, he argued:

> The goal of the first period is the overthrow of the despotic [French colonial] government, where the people have been bestialised, dehumanised, exploited and subjugated . . .
>
> The goal of the second period is the intensive exploitation of the triumph of the revolution. Thus, after having kicked the French out of our borders, we must destroy the counterrevolutionary elements, build roads for transportation and communication, develop commerce and industry, educate the people, and provide them with peace and happiness.
>
> (HO CHI MINH WRITING IN THE JOURNAL *THANH NIEN*, QUOTED IN HUYNH KIM KHANH, *VIETNAMESE COMMUNISM 1925–1945*, 1982)

For both Ho and Hatta, and for thousands of other early modern nationalists in the colonised regions of Southeast Asia who came to learn about the nature of government in the West, the most striking realisation was how different were the patterns of life and behaviour in Europe and the United States. The colonialists' assumption of superiority led to resentment, and this resentment was further fuelled by the realisation that the bulk of the economic benefits associated with the colonies were not enjoyed by their indigenous populations. Awareness of the unequal nature of colonial rule was, for most of those active in the developing nationalist movements, increasingly focused on these two features: the social and political dominance of the alien colonialists over the indigenous population and the economic dominance of those colonists.

Having recognised a link between the colonial political systems and the economic situation in the colonies, thoughtful Southeast Asian nationalists asked whether Western political and economic theory might offer an answer to their problems. Following the 1917 Communist Revolution in Russia, it's not surprising that some saw the revolutionary theories of communism as a way of gaining independence. If a political group acting in the name of the workers of Russia could overthrow a corrupt, authoritarian monarchy, perhaps embracing communism could lead to the overthrow of colonial regimes.

The role of communism in the developing anti-colonial movements in Southeast Asia was most important in Vietnam, but communism also had its followers in Indonesia and played a small but significant role in the Philippines. In British Malaya, communist organisers were active in the Chinese community, but in this case it was to gain support for their communist countrymen in China rather than to work against British control of Malaya. Yet the question remains—why was it only in Vietnam that a belief in communism and the fight for national independence became inseparably linked? Some of the answers to this question can be gained by comparing the men who became the leaders of the independence movements in Vietnam and Indonesia, the only two countries that had to fight protracted wars to gain their independence.

The leaders of the small but determined Vietnamese Communist Party in the 1930s were men of exceptional talent and a readiness to eliminate ruthlessly those of their countrymen who did not share their views, even if these Vietnamese were, themselves, opponents of French rule. The defeats the anti-colonial movements—in the form of major rural revolts—suffered in the 1930–31 period did not deter them; neither did the readiness of the French authorities to jail and execute convicted and suspected revolutionaries. Men such as Ho Chi Minh believed that communism, particularly as developed by the Russian leader, Lenin, provided both a political theory and a program for action that was particularly suited to the colonial conditions that existed in Vietnam. Moreover, in embracing communism, the Vietnamese who campaigned for independence did so in the belief that the old, Confucian values of traditional Vietnamese society had failed totally. For the Vietnamese communists, the ideas of Marx and

Lenin provided an all-embracing ideology to replace the past Confucian systems of thought that were clearly so inadequate.

There were believers in communism in Indonesia, too, but they were only one element in the emerging Indonesian nationalist movement where many of the leaders had strong links with Islam. Moreover, in Indonesia there was no similar belief that the traditional values of the past had to be abandoned. The best-known of the leaders of the Indonesian independence movement, Sukarno, makes this point very clearly. He was seen by his followers as representing many, if not all, of the characteristics and values of his compatriots, particularly his fellow Javanese. By birth he was from an aristocratic family, in a society where rank mattered. If his manner was more forceful than that of the calm Javanese stereotype, Sukarno always showed himself acutely aware of traditional values, including emphasising the mystical importance of the date of his birth. At the same time, and as the result of a remarkable knowledge of Western political writings, he looked for a path to Indonesian independence that took account of the widest range of ideas of how government should function. Nationalism in Indonesia was able to accommodate a range of political views. In Vietnam, the movement for independence was, by the end of the 1930s, overwhelmingly linked to communism.

Sukarno was brought to trial by the Dutch in August 1930 under a piece of 'catch-all' colonial legislation charging him with 'disturbing public tranquillity'. His speech in his own defence lasted two days and made clear his embrace of forward-looking nationalism:

> There is no people who can attain greatness without national independence, there is no country that can be firm and strong without being free. Conversely, no colony can attain glory; no colony can attain greatness . . . Every people which lacks freedom, every people which because it is unable to control its own affairs in its own interests and for its own happiness lives in an unsettled atmosphere . . .
>
> (QUOTED IN J.D. LEGGE, *SUKARNO: A POLITICAL BIOGRAPHY,* 1985)

President Sukarno was the first leader of independent Indonesia. Active as a revolutionary from the 1920s, Sukarno was a man of remarkable talents mixed with personal weaknesses. Between 1946 and 1965 Sukarno dominated Indonesian domestic politics and played a prominent role in international affairs. (PHOTOGRAPH BY DEREK DAVIES COURTESY OF *FAR EASTERN ECONOMIC REVIEW*)

Religion and nationalism

The closer one looks at the rise of nationalism in Southeast Asia, the more it becomes clear that a wide range of factors help to explain the way in which it developed. There were events in other regions of the world that were seen as providing possible models for action. The Russian revolution has just been mentioned, but Southeast Asians certainly also took note of the Chinese revolution of 1911, and of the fact that Japan defeated Russia in the Russo–Japanese War of 1905. This latter event was seen as important because it showed that an Asian country could defeat a European power. In terms of factors that were important within Southeast Asian countries themselves, the role of religion certainly deserves emphasis.

In Indonesia, the first truly important national organisation linked Islam to the economic interests of *batik* cloth merchants under the name Sarekat Islam (Islamic Association). These merchants came together because of their concerns about competition from Chinese traders, and found a sense of unity and identity in their shared religion. For many Indonesians who joined Sarekat Islam in its early, essentially economic phase, and for others who through the 1920s and 1930s associated themselves with other Islamic organisations, their religion became more than a simple statement of personal belief. The fact of being a follower of Islam became a political statement as well. And in Malaya, from the beginning of the twentieth century, Islam played a similar, if less significant, role in emphasising the common interests of followers of this faith throughout the Peninsula.

Another religion, Buddhism, provided a central rallying point for the emerging nationalist movement in Burma between the two world wars. It would be wrong to suggest that there was the same level of agitation for independence in Burma as there was in Vietnam and Indonesia, but an active nationalist movement certainly existed and within it Buddhism was seen as setting Burmans apart from alien non-Buddhist Asians, such as the Indians who had flocked to Burma after the establishment of British rule. What is more, the religion provided an administrative framework for the nationalists to spread their ideas. Propaganda in favour of independence could be circulated within the monkhood and anti-colonial strategies could be discussed at Buddhist councils.

So, as was the case with Islam in Indonesia, Buddhism in Burma played a role for the nationalists that affirmed national identity as well as giving spiritual comfort to its followers.

Accepting the status quo

The attention given to Indonesia, Vietnam and, to a lesser extent Burma, reflects the fact that nationalist stirrings were not so apparent in the rest of Southeast Asia. Indeed, in Cambodia and the Lao states in the 1920s and 1930s, there simply were no significant nationalist movements. In both these countries—and in considerable contrast to Vietnam, the other French colony in Indochina—traditional society and the traditional ruling class were preserved under the control of the French administration. The Cambodian and Lao rulers still had a vital role in the eyes of their subjects and showed no wish to change their relationships with the French. Moreover, in contrast to the spread of Western education in both Indonesia and Vietnam, modern political ideas had virtually no impact in either Cambodia or Laos where at the end of the 1930s only a handful of students had completed high school education.

Given its long history as a colony, and the anti-Spanish movements at the end of the nineteenth century, one would have expected a more active nationalist movement in the Philippines than was the case. The explanation for the lack of a vigorous call for independence seems linked to two facts. With the United States granting a large measure of self-government under a 'Commonwealth' arrangement, Filipinos, by and large, accepted the promise of the United States that it was, indeed, determined to grant independence. Second, the country's elite who might have been most likely to press for independence found their economic interests were well-served by a system that allowed an active political life under generally benign American control.

European attitudes to independence

Looking back at Southeast Asia's history during the 1920s and 1930s, it is striking to see that, with the exception of the American promise of independence for the Philippines, most of those who administered the other colonial regimes seem to have been convinced that they would remain in place indefinitely. Arrogance certainly provides part of the explanation for this attitude. European, and to a lesser extent American, colonial officials *believed* they had a right to rule. Sometimes genuinely, and sometimes self-deludingly, they justified their actions in terms of Rudyard Kipling's words of 'taking up the White Man's burden'. Of course, self-interest linked to economic advantage was involved, but this was not all. Men such as Frank Swettenham, one of Britain's best-known colonial administrators, wrote in 1927 of bringing colonised people 'from the dark shadow into which their days were passed into the daylight of personal freedom such as white men prize above most mundane things'. Yet Swettenham and most other colonialists did not see that without independence a degree of personal freedom was not enough.

Moreover, there was what might be called a practical reason for the views the colonialists held. Apart from major rural revolts against French rule in Vietnam in 1930–31 mentioned earlier, all of the other challenges to colonial governments were essentially short-term in character and easily overcome. Not only that, the various challenges that did emerge, including communist-led risings against Dutch rule in the Netherlands Indies, were still heavily marked by traditional overtones, including appeals to magic. This was the case with the Saya San rising in Burma in 1930–31, in which peasant protesters thought they would be protected against police bullets by chanting magic spells and wearing sacred amulets. Similarly, the 1926 protests against Dutch rule in Sumatra could be dismissed as having little modern political, let alone nationalist, significance because of the unrealistic claims that went hand in hand with practical demands. (The protesters called for free taxi rides and claimed that the Turkish leader, Kemal Attaturk, was about to arrive by plane to lead the protesters to victory.) As a result, and despite some vague thought being given by the British to the eventual possibility of an independent Burma, at the end of the 1930s, the Philippines was the only colonial possession in which independence was a goal accepted by colonisers and colonised alike.

The 1930s: A decade of uncertainty

If the 1920s were a period of relative stability throughout Southeast Asia, the following decade was marked by a sense of uncertainty. Southeast Asia did not escape the effects of the Great Depression that burst upon the Western industrialised world at the beginning of the 1930s. The Great Depression is often thought of in terms of the massive unemployment that plagued the West, but it had a dramatic impact in Southeast Asia as well. It was a time when the markets for rubber, tin and rice collapsed, so that the export economies of the region were temporarily crippled and employment opportunities for hundreds of thousands of Southeast Asians vanished.

In the broadest terms, too, the 1930s were a time when it became apparent that economic change had been accompanied by the rise of serious social problems. In some areas of Java and in Vietnam, there were clear problems of overpopulation, which meant there was an ever-present risk of famine. And social inequalities were sharpened as a relatively small number of Southeast Asians prospered from the presence of colonial rule.

Coupled with the emergence of modern nationalist movements was a more general sense of change among the colonial peoples throughout Southeast Asia. Awareness of this sense of change varied from country to country, but by the end of the 1930s, the population of the region knew more about the outside world, more about the extent to which the colonial powers depended on their distant possessions for prosperity, and more about the basic inequality between ruler and ruled in the colonies. None of this meant that the colonised populations were all straining for independence and ready for revolt just before the Second World War began. But the numbers of Southeast Asians who had come to believe that change must take place had grown substantially. Even among the peasantry, who had no knowledge of modern political theories, there was an awareness that change was taking place. And for the small but growing number of educated Southeast Asians, an awareness of the dramatic events taking place in China, of the growth in power of another Asian country, Japan, and of resistance to British rule in India, all acted to encourage a desire for change.

We cannot be sure how much of this change in attitude was recognised by the European colonisers as a threat to their position. In fact, everything suggests that only a few ever contemplated the possibility that the colonies in which they served would be independent in a relatively short time. For the others, the majority, the illusion of continuity blinded them to the great changes that had taken place in just over twenty years and to their potential consequences. With the notable exception of the Philippines, where the Americans were committed to granting independence, and with Thailand distinctively uncolonised, those who ruled the countries of Southeast Asia had no expectation that independence would be granted in their own lifetimes. This fact was reflected in the colonisers' actions, both large and small. It was apparent in the limitations placed on political action, that meant colonised peoples were restricted from making decisions on their own behalf, and it was reflected in the way that 'natives' were excluded from the clubs, the all-important gathering places of European colonial society. And so as they sipped their sundowners at the end of the day, the colonialists believed they were secure in their role. When change did come it was to be of a character more shocking than any of the colonisers had anticipated.

8

The Second World War in Southeast Asia

As the 1930s drew to a close, there was no widespread expectation among the still-small number of Southeast Asian nationalists that the colonial administrations which controlled every country in the region except Thailand might soon be dramatically challenged. Whatever their hopes, independence still seemed a distant goal for even the most dedicated nationalists. The Philippines was a separate case, for there independence was regarded as not too far-distant, and in Burma, there was inconclusive discussion about possible self-government, not independence. But in the other British, Dutch and French colonies, the idea of independence was generally not even discussed by the colonial rulers. Nowhere was this clearer than in the Netherlands East Indies, where, in the 1930s, Governor-General de Jonge firmly insisted that the Dutch would be ruling their colonial subjects for another three hundred years.

It was this kind of outlook that explains why the Second World War had such a shattering impact on Southeast Asia, on Southeast Asians, and on the colonial administrators who served in the region. More than anything else, the Second World War in Southeast Asia marked a point of no return, a period that ensured the old pattern of European dominance could never be re-established. For the Japanese invasion of Southeast Asia was not just a military event, or series of events. It was a political bombshell that shattered the views and attitudes underpinning the whole colonial relationship between ruler and ruled.

Above all, the Japanese victories in Southeast Asia showed that the arguments of the various nationalist groups in the colonies had been right—the colonial powers and their representatives *could* be defeated by Asians. And not only defeated. Following their defeat, the white-skinned aliens were toppled from their privileged position in society to become no better off than the coolies who had laboured at the beck and call of colonial society during the years of peace. Even for those Southeast Asians who had no strong nationalist feelings the fact that the myth of European superiority could be demolished almost overnight was of vital importance. The world of Southeast Asia could never be the same again. In the words of a Southeast Asian writer commenting later on this period, the world had been turned upside down.

The Japanese advance

In a period of months, the Japanese heaped humiliation upon humiliation on the colonial powers. In French Indochina, before the outbreak of the Pacific War—heralded by the Japanese attack on Pearl Harbor in December 1941—the Japanese had already established a position in which they held the real reins of power. As the Japanese mustered their military might in Indochina in 1941, they allowed the French administration to continue operating. But the French now held their position at the will of the Japanese, a fact that was not lost on the growing number of politically conscious Vietnamese, and was apparent even to the still-small number of nationalists in Cambodia and Laos.

The conquest of Malaya and Singapore in 1942 involved an even greater humiliation. Years of planning neglect and an appalling unreadiness on the part of British service chiefs to face up to the reality of Japanese power led to a debacle of the most staggering kind. Dismissed by British planners as ill-trained and incompetent, Japanese troops moved rapidly down the Malayan Peninsula driving the badly led British and Commonwealth forces before them until they had the overcrowded island of Singapore, the population swollen with refugees, the main water supply from Malaya cut off, at their mercy. Singapore fell to the Japanese on 15 February 1942.

After the defeat of the British in Malay and Singapore, it was the turn of the Dutch to face defeat in Indonesia. The Battle of the Java Sea, at the end of February 1942, ensured the capitulation of the Dutch and allied forces in Java and then the surrender of Dutch forces in nearly all of Indonesia by the end of March. In little more than than three months, Japan was in military control of the countries of French Indochina, the British possessions in Malaya, Singapore and Borneo, almost all of the Netherlands Indies (Indonesia) and was occupying Portuguese Timor (East Timor).

Thailand retained its independence at the cost of allowing the Japanese to move troops through its territory, but this was a different situation from what was occurring in French Indochina, for it remained clear that Thai sovereignty was not in question. Only Burma and the Philippines had still not come under full Japanese military control at the end of March 1942. Bitter fighting by American and Philippine forces delayed a Japanese victory in the Philippines until the first half of May 1942. And in Burma, fighting dragged on into July as British, Indian and Chinese troops fought to escape the invading Japanese forces.

The speed of these events, with the greater part of Southeast Asia falling to the Japanese in less than six months of fighting, had never been expected by the colonial powers; it amazed the

Well before the Japanese captured Singapore in February 1942, the largely Chinese civilian population suffered heavy casualities from bombing. In this photograph, two Chinese women react to the cost of the bombing in terms of lives and destruction. Once the Japanese entered Singapore they wreaked a savage retribution on those local Chinese who they believed were hostile to them. (PHOTOGRAPH COURTESY OF THE AUSTRALIAN WAR MEMORIAL NEGATIVE NO. 11529/22)

Japanese themselves, who had anticipated more effective resistance. With the old colonial masters removed and their prestige damaged beyond repair, the people in much of Southeast Asia found that they now had new colonial masters, Asians this time, it's true, but in other ways, occupying the same sort of position as those they had just defeated. Leaving aside independent Thailand and the curious situation in Vietnam, Cambodia and Laos, the rest of Southeast Asia saw one alien sovereignty removed to make way for control by another.

Only in Burma was there an effort by members of the nationalist movement to associate themselves with the advancing Japanese forces. When the Japanese marched into Burma, they were accompanied by members of the Burma Independence Army (BIA). Numbering barely a thousand when the Japanese invasion began in January 1942, its numbers grew as the advance moved steadily forward. But even at the end of the Burma campaign, when the BIA claimed a membership approaching 30 000, the Japanese gave no sign of giving the BIA's leaders any real power. In Burma, as elsewhere, Japan saw its interests as supreme, and rapidly revealed the hollowness of earlier propaganda that spoke of an 'Asian Co-Prosperity Sphere' and called for 'Asia for the Asians'.

Japanese rule in Southeast Asia

Although the Japanese who occupied the countries of Southeast Asia filled a role that was similar in many ways to that of the old colonial powers, there were important differences. At the beginning of Japanese rule, there was much that the Japanese did and said that was welcomed by many indigenous Southeast Asians.

Malaya and Singapore

While the Japanese meted out savage treatment to thousands of ethnic Chinese in Singapore and Malaya, seeing them as untrustworthy supporters of the Chinese armies still fighting the Japanese in China itself, their treatment of Malays in Malaya was very different. In that country, the Japanese tried to gain the support of the Malays by showing careful respect for the traditional rulers, the sultans, and by appointing Malays to positions of prominence, if not power.

Indonesia

Having defeated the Dutch in Indonesia, the Japanese released the many Indonesian nationalists who had been languishing in colonial prisons, some for more than a decade. On their release, some of these nationalists, Sukarno and Hatta being among the most prominent, decided that they could best achieve their long-held goal of independence by working with the Japanese. From the nationalists' point of view, this was a sensible strategy—for them, the Japanese were liberators. But their readiness to work with the invaders later bedevilled relations between the Indonesians and the Dutch when the Japanese were finally defeated. Many Dutch came to regard men such as Sukarno as collaborators with the enemy whose actions were a further reason to oppose the nationalists' demands for independence.

It was not long before Indonesians came to recognise that the Japanese, like the Dutch, were not ready to allow them to rule themselves. Nevertheless, the Japanese gave the Indonesians greater opportunity than they had ever enjoyed before to develop political organisations and, most importantly, to promote the symbols of a future independent state. Indonesians could assemble beneath a national flag and sing songs calling for independence. At the same time, the Japanese provided young Indonesians with new models of behaviour. Old values of deference towards elders and of dislike of violence began to be questioned. The realisation that aggression could play its part in achieving political goals was to be of the greatest importance when the nationalists' found they would have to fight for their independence once the war was over.

Burma

In Burma, the Japanese adopted a different approach to that which they followed in Indonesia. Initially, the Japanese were ready to sponsor the establishment of a Burmese administration headed by a well-known older nationalist, Ba Maw, and there was a widespread Burmese expectation that this meant the Japanese would pay due attention to Burmese interests. But these Burmese hopes were misplaced and from late 1942 onwards, distrust between Burmese and Japanese grew as it became clear that Japan's interests would always override those of the Burmese. It also became obvious that Japanese claims to be respectful of Burmese Buddhism, the most valued symbol of Burmese identity, were hollow. The Japanese, the Burmese recognised, were simply trying to use their statements of respect for Buddhism to further their political and military goals.

Despite allowing the Burmese administration to proclaim 'independence' in 1943, the Japanese demands on the Burmese population became ever greater. They were required to provide food and war materials. Then, most disturbingly of all, they had to provide coolie labour to work on the strategic road and rail projects that the Japanese were building to support their war effort. Growing resentment of these demands and a realisation that the Japanese had no intention of allowing Burma to enjoy real independence led to the formation of a secret organisation of Burmese who were ready to oppose the Japanese once the fortunes of war started running against them. As it finally became evident that the Japanese were facing defeat, these same Burmese planned to work for independence once the British returned and sought to rule Burma as before.

The Philippines

The other country to experience the granting of 'independence' while the result of the war in the Pacific and Southeast Asia was still undecided was the Philippines. When the American and Philippine forces were defeated by the Japanese in 1942, a large number of the pre-war Commonwealth period politicians decided to cooperate with the conquering Japanese. Because the Philippines had moved so far towards independence before the war began, the administration that rallied to the Japanese should have been a much more effective body than was the case in Burma. This was not what happened. The politicians and their elite associates who chose to work with the Japanese never succeeded in seeming other than puppets. Moreover, the mass of the population remained hostile to the occupying power. This hostility was reinforced as the Japanese behaved brutally towards civilians and made heavy demands on them for labour and supplies. The proclamation of

Philippines 'independence' did nothing to transform the situation as, in the same way as elsewhere in Southeast Asia, it became ever clearer that Japanese interests overrode all others. This fact led to the development of an active anti-Japanese guerrilla movement that carried out hit-and-run strikes against the occupiers.

Yet as the war drew to a close, the scale of cooperation with the Japanese—or collaboration in the eyes of the guerrillas—was so great among the Philippine elite that once peace came, there was an acceptance that little would be served by trying to punish or exclude from public life those who had been ready to work with the Japanese. All the same, memories of this period of modern Philippines history left bitter divisions for many years within the country's society.

Vietnam

Unlike the other European powers in Southeast Asia, the rulers of French Indochina—Vietnam, Cambodia and Laos—had not fought against the advancing Japanese. Instead, with France itself under German occupation, the French in Indochina struck an agreement with the Japanese. The Japanese were allowed to move troops through Indochina and to make use of local facilities such as airfields, and in return the French were permitted to continue administering their colonial possessions as before. This arrangement was presented by the French administrators of the time as a successful way to maintain French sovereignty.

In fact, such a claim was largely a sham. While the French administration throughout Indochina continued to function much as before, it did so entirely at the pleasure of the Japanese, who increasingly placed heavy demands on the local population for the provision of food, strategic supplies and manpower. It was a situation that played into the hands of the still-small but growing communist movement. With Ho Chi Minh directing their efforts, the communists steadily developed a range of front organisations that emphasised the nationalist goal of independence as much as communist ideology. The most important of these front organisations was the Viet Minh (the Vietnamese Independence Brotherhood League). At the same time, and with ruthless efficiency, Ho and his lieutenants worked to undermine, and if necessary eliminate, other Vietnamese nationalists who did not share their views.

Ho Chi Minh spent much of the Second World War in China, first as a prisoner in Chinese jails and then as a key figure in organising an anti-French front movement before returning to Vietnam in August 1944. While in jail, he wrote a series of poems, later published in English translation as his *Prison Diary*. Many of the poems, originally written in classical Chinese, emphasise his longing to return to Vietnam:

> My heart travels a thousand *li* towards my native land,
> My dream intertwines with sadness like a skein of a thousand threads,
> Innocent, I now endure a whole year in prison,
> Using my tears for ink, I turn my thoughts into verse.
>
> (FROM *AUTUMN NIGHT*)

Then, as the tide of war flowed steadily against them, the Japanese forces in the countries of Indochina made a last throw of the dice in the hope of bolstering their position and maintaining their control over this economically and strategically important region. In March 1945, they seized control of the administration throughout Indochina, interning the French officials who had held their pre-war positions up to this time. In Vietnam, the Japanese seizure of power was followed shortly after by their sponsoring the proclamation of Vietnam's 'independence' under the leadership of Emperor Bao Dai.

The 'independent' state of Vietnam was no more than a device to disguise Japanese domination of the country, and this was recognised by almost all politically conscious Vietnamese. But with the removal of the French administrators, it became possible for the communist-led Viet Minh forces to accelerate their military and political efforts to seize power. They knew they could not defeat the Japanese, but they were working with the aim of confronting the French once the Japanese were defeated. Although they were not the only Vietnamese who wanted independence from the French, it seems undeniable that the communist-led forces were the most able and effective, not least through their use of brute force, of the Vietnamese groups jockeying for power ahead of a French return.

Cambodia and Laos

Events in Cambodia and Laos did not have the same high drama that marked the closing stages of the Second World War in Vietnam. Important events took place, it's true, as Cambodia's king, Norodom Sihanouk, proclaimed 'independence' for his country, and as a limited number of Lao demonstrated their determination to resist the return of France as a colonial power. But in both these countries the traditional leaders had, in general, linked their fortunes with the French administration in the period before the war and were happy enough to see the French return. The brief experience of a period without French colonial direction—after March 1945 until the end of the war in August of the same year—was not sufficient to set the stage for the sort of conflict that developed in Vietnam. Individuals who became prominent at this time were important in the future, but for the moment, most of the elite contemplated the return of the French without regret.

The end of the war

The war ended in a different fashion in each of the countries of Southeast Asia. In Burma and the Philippines, the Japanese experienced military defeat at the hands of allied forces. Throughout the rest of the region, the war came to an end with

Japan surrendered on 15 August 1945 to end the Pacific War and its occupation of the countries of Southeast Asia. The Allied Supreme Commander for the Pacific, General Douglas MacArthur, formally accepted the Japanese surrender aboard the USS Missouri *in Tokoyo Bay on 2 September 1945. The Japanese surrender meant the victory of the colonial powers that had controlled Southeast Asia before the Second World War, but the defeat those powers had suffered in 1942 ensured that the colonial era could never again be reinstituted without challenge.* (PHOTOGRAPH COURTESY OF THE AUSTRALIAN WAR MEMORIAL NEGATIVE NO. 19128)

the Japanese still in control of the populations of the countries they occupied. Once again, Thailand was an exception, for its astute politicians managed to align themselves with the victorious allied forces as the war came to an end.

The details of this complex period are less important than a recognition of the fact that, whatever the expectations of the colonial powers of resuming 'business as usual' after the Japanese defeat, the Second World War had shattered forever the former relationship between colonisers and colonised. There could never be a return to the past. For all the countries of Southeast Asia, the next decades were dominated by the issue of independence, how it would be granted or resisted, and whether it would be gained by violence or in peace.

PART II

Gaining
independence:
Common goals,
individual histories

9

Revolution and revolt

The various states of modern Southeast Asia gained their independence in different ways and over an extended period of time. In some cases, notably in Indonesia and Vietnam, independence was gained only after prolonged armed struggle against the colonial powers. In the case of the Philippines, the newly independent government had to confront a serious armed challenged from communist insurgents. Yet again, Malaya gained independence while still fighting an ethnically based insurgency. This chapter considers these various examples of revolution and revolt in Southeast Asia.

Indonesia

The history of the Indonesian revolution has always commanded attention, not least because of the country's status as the largest state in Southeast Asia. But other reasons have led to widespread interest, in particular, the spectacle that the revolution provided of an economically poor and militarily weak nation seeking freedom from colonial control against daunting odds.

When the war ended with the Japanese surrender, British troops were the first allied forces to land in Indonesia, arriving in September 1945. By this time, Sukarno with Hatta at his side had proclaimed Indonesia's independence, on 17 August 1945 at a ceremony in Jakarta. This was a highly symbolic act of defiance, for it was known that the Dutch planned to return and that the British forces landing in Java were intended to back the reimposition of Dutch colonial control. In an event that signalled the readiness of Indonesians to fight for their goal of independence, forces loyal to the newly proclaimed Indonesian state opposed the British occupation of the major Javanese port city of Surabaya in a battle that took a heavy toll of casualties on both sides.

Nevertheless, when Dutch administrators returned to Indonesia in early 1946, there was no guarantee that the Indonesian nationalists would be able to translate their declaration of independence into the reality of a new state. Still militarily weak, the leading nationalists initially were ready to enter into negotiations with the Dutch, who at this stage appeared ready to talk about the possibility of future independence. But by the end of 1946, it was clear that a great gap separated the two sides. For the Indonesian leadership, negotiations could only be concerned with the rapid achievement of independence. For the Dutch, trapped into a way of thinking that reflected their colonial background, what was under discussion was the *eventual* granting of independence to Indonesia at some future, and probably distant, date. At the same time the Dutch tried to strengthen their position by lending their support to representatives from the outer Indonesian islands who held concerns about being dominated by an independent Indonesian government based in Java.

As negotiations bogged down over issues of basic principle with both sides concluding that their opponents were acting in bad faith, the Dutch launched what they described as a 'police action' in July 1947. In military terms—for it was a military not a police campaign that the Dutch mounted—the former colonial power had some success. They gained control over vital areas of Java and Sumatra and were able to deny food supplies to the nationalist troops. This apparent 'success' proved to be hollow. The readiness of the Dutch to try and impose their will by force led to an increased determination on the part of the Indonesian nationalists to settle for nothing less than full independence. At the same time, the Dutch actions convinced those Indonesians who had previously argued in favour of accepting something short of immediate independence that this was no longer an acceptable course of action.

The 'police action' had other consequences, most importantly in shaping international opinion, expressed through the newly established United Nations, critical of the Dutch. Although the Dutch position continued to receive support from other colonial powers such as Britain and France, the United States was less committed to the former colonial power, and pressure from the United Nations brought a halt to the 1947 police action. Once again, negotiations were resumed, and once again, as these failed to bring an agreed result, the Dutch mounted another police action at the end of 1948.

As with the first police action, Dutch military gains did not lead to a weakening of the nationalist cause. The reverse occurred as more and more Indonesians rallied to the independence cause. Moreover, by this stage it was clear that any ideas that the Dutch held of being able to maintain their position through support from the outer islands was doomed to fail. With increasing international pressure for an end to the conflict, an agreement was finally reached for the full transfer of sovereignty to an independent Indonesian government at the end of 1949. Under this agreement, Indonesia gained control of all of the territories of the former Netherlands East Indies with the exception of West New Guinea (Irian Jaya or Papua). Its status was to be determined at a later date.

Two developments that occurred during the Indonesian revolution deserve particular attention. The first involved the Indonesian Communist Party, the second an extremist Islamic sect, the Darul Islam. To the present day, both developments have remained important in Indonesian minds.

During the Indonesian revolution, the communists were only one of the many political parties that joined together on the nationalist side. They were not, in great contrast to Vietnam, the leading element in the nationalist struggle. Pursuing their own political interests, elements within the Communist Party attempted a takeover of the revolutionary movement in September 1948, operating from their base at Madiun in central Java. It was an attempt that ended in bitter failure after less than a month as the best troops in the Indonesian revolutionary army ruthlessly crushed the communists, who were seen as undermining the nationalist cause. The Madiun Affair, as this event has been known ever since, left shock waves that still agitate the surface of Indonesian politics. Above all, the Madiun Affair left the army and its leaders convinced that the communists could not be trusted to put the national interest above their party's political aspirations.

The other notable challenge to the emerging Indonesian political leadership came from the Darul Islam. This extremist Islamic group was committed to the ideal of Indonesia as an Islamic state, a concept that had been decisively rejected by the leading figures of the nationalist movement. Drawing support from those regions where adherence to Islam was strongest, such as West Java, northern Sumatra and parts of Kalimantan (Borneo), Darul Islam tried to gain control of territory to advance its position at the time of the second Dutch 'police action'. As was the case with the Madiun Affair, this action was seen by the nationalists as a betrayal and was met with determined force.

The challenge and defeat of the communists and the Darul Islam showed that the Indonesian revolutionary government opposing the Dutch was ready to use harsh measures to maintain its internal position. At the same time, throughout the revolutionary period the Indonesian army's use of guerrilla warfare tactics showed that they could not be defeated by the better-equipped Dutch forces. The role of the Indonesian army throughout this 1946–49 period gave it a very special place within Indonesian society. This is not as strong as it was in the past, but the military still have an important *political* role in contemporary Indonesia.

With independence gained in December 1949, Indonesia faced formidable problems. While the men who had led the revolution, such as Sukarno and Hatta, were initially assured of popular support, they now had to face the reality of a massive debt to the Dutch, the difficulties associated with administering a nation scattered throughout an island archipelago, and the need to find a political system that could serve the interests of a growing population that had never experienced independent government before. Faced with these challenges, it is not surprising that the feeling of optimism that accompanied the achievement of independence rapidly vanished in the years immediately after the Dutch departed.

Vietnam

As memories of the wars fought in Vietnam after the Second World War begin to fade, there is a risk that outside observers will increasingly fail to understand the enormity of the scale and human cost of the the revolutionary struggle that took place in that country between 1945 and 1975. This is particularly so in the case of the Vietnamese war against the French, fought between 1946 and 1954, a war which remains comparatively little-known. This earlier conflict has been overshadowed by the events associated with the Second Indochina War, the 'American' war in Vietnam, fought between the late 1950s and 1975. But unless what happened in the years between 1946 and 1954 is understood, it is impossible to gain a true sense of why the Vietnamese communists should have fought for so long to achieve their goals when the French were no longer their enemies.

At the beginning of September 1945, and before a huge crowd in Hanoi, Ho Chi Minh proclaimed the independence of Vietnam under a provisional government dominated by the Viet Minh, and so by the Vietnamese Communist Party. Yet despite the excitement of the occasion, Ho knew he was in no position to prevent the return of the French. In southern Vietnam, British troops prepared the way for the eventual re-establishment of the colonial administration, while in the north of the country the task of disarming the occupying Japanese was given to Chinese Nationalist troops. Faced with this situation, Ho and his lieutenants worked to strengthen their political position while entering into negotiations with the returning French.

At the time he proclaimed Vietnam's independence, Ho Chi Minh hoped that he could enlist the support of the United States to aid his position. To this end, his 'Declaration of Independence' began with words drawn from the American Declaration of Independence. Ho also drew on the words of the French Declaration on the Rights of Man. What follows are the early paragraphs of the Vietnamese Declaration:

All men are created equal. They are endowed by their creator with certain inalienable rights, among these are Life, Liberty and the Pursuit of Happiness.

This immortal statement was made in the Declaration of Independence of the United States of America in 1776. In a broader sense, this means: All peoples on earth are equal from birth, all peoples have the right to live, to be happy, to be free.

The Declaration of the French Revolution made in 1791 on the Rights of Man and the Citizen also states: 'All men are born free and with equal rights, and must always remain free and have equal rights.'

These are undeniable truths.

Nevertheless, for more than eighty years, the French imperialists, abusing the standard of Liberty, Equality and Fraternity,

have violated our Fatherland and oppressed our fellow-citizens. They
have acted contrary to the ideals of humanity and justice.

(HO CHI MINH, *SELECTED WORKS*, 1961)

Like the Dutch in Indonesia, the French entered into these
negotiations with the basic aim of re-establishing their pre-war
position. Since the Vietnamese negotiators had no other aim than
full independence from France, war became inevitable. It began with
a series of guerrilla engagements, but by the closing phases of the
war it was a conflict fought at all levels, from main-force battles
to local skirmishes. It was, from the Vietnamese communists' point
of view, a highly political war. Defeating the French was a goal to
be achieved through all possible means. So the Viet Minh worked
to undermine French control at every level, setting up a parallel
administration alongside that of the French. This meant they could
collect taxes both in the areas under their direct control and in
areas that were, supposedly, under French control. And since they
saw the war as part of a broader political struggle, they pursued
other goals that, at first glance, seem surprising. As an example,
the Viet Minh embarked on a literacy campaign, so that the
population could better understand the written propaganda
justifying the battle against the French.

The strength of the Vietnamese fighting against the French
was greatest in the north of the country, but this did not mean
that the Viet Minh was inactive elsewhere. Rather, it was the case
that the nature of the war fought between 1946 and 1954 varied
between the large battles fought in the north and the largely
guerrilla operations that took place in the south. The truth of this
situation was confirmed in the war maps of the French high
command, which in 1954 showed large areas of southern Vietnam
in the hands of the Viet Minh.

In the early phases of the war, the French had an overwhelming
superiority in men and equipment. What they did not have was
an indefinite amount of time to re-estabish their colonial control.
The leaders of the Viet Minh knew this, so their strategy was to

prolong the war in the knowledge that this would eventually result in French domestic opinion seeking an end to the conflict. Although the French were able to return to Hanoi and Saigon and to keep major rail and road links open, this did not mean that French military forces could eliminate the challenge posed by the Viet Minh's guerillas. Under the increasingly able leadership of General Vo Nguyen Giap, the Vietnamese mostly struck only when the odds were in their favour before slipping away into the mountains and jungles where the French troops could not follow them.

It was not the case that the Viet Minh were always invincible, and there were times when Giap made serious military mistakes, particular in the period 1950–51. But by 1953, it was increasingly clear that the French had no prospect of defeating the Viet Minh. What was now uncertain was whether the Viet Minh could, for their part, defeat the French. The issue was resolved at the Battle of Dien Bien Phu, fought between March and May 1954.

At the end of 1953, the French high command remained convinced that if their opponents could be drawn into a major, set-piece battle, better-armed French forces could inflict a decisive defeat on the enemy. This conviction led to the French establishing themselves at Dien Bien Phu, in northern Vietnam, in the belief that they would be able to defeat any Viet Minh force that was thrown against them. With hindsight, the folly of this French decision seems extraordinary, as does their estimation of the forces and equipment the Viet Minh would be able to direct against them. Critically, the valley chosen by the French to concentrate their troops in was at the very limit of air supply from Hanoi and was poorly suited for the construction of bunkers. Even more seriously, given these facts, the French had concluded that the Viet Minh would not be able to bring artillery through the rugged mountains surrounding Dien Bien Phu to use in a siege of their position.

When the battle was joined, both sides recognised the vital importance of the outcome, and both displayed remarkable courage and endurance under near-intolerable conditions. When the Viet Minh forces finally overran the French positions, their success had

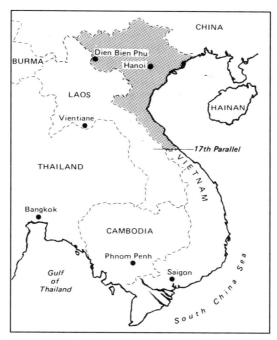

Vietnam at the end of the First Indochina War
The French defeat at Dien Bien Phu in May 1954 sealed the end of France's colonial position in Vietnam. Following the Geneva Conference that ended in July 1954, Ho Chi Minh's Viet Minh gained control of norther Vietnam down to the 17th parallel and an American-backed state was established in the south.

cost them dearly, their casualties being far in excess of those on the French side. But for the Viet Minh, this was a price worth paying, for the French defeat at Dien Bien Phu heralded the end of French rule in Vietnam. With two months of their defeat at Dien Bien Phu, the French had joined in negotiations in Geneva that led to a fragile peace and the temporary partition of Vietnam at the seventeenth parallel.

Lacking support from the Soviet Union and China, the major communist powers, the Vietnamese communists were forced to settle for control of half the country, with an anti-communist regime supported by the United States in place in the south of the country. For the communists, the revolution had only half succeeded, but there is no doubt that they were confident that full success would soon be theirs. When peace came temporarily to Vietnam, few if any observers realised just how high would be the cost before the communists finally did achieve their goal of controlling the whole of Vietnam's territory twenty-one years later.

The Philippines

The revolutionary struggles in Indonesia and Vietnam were not matched elsewhere in Southeast Asia, but this did not mean that the post-war period was universally peaceful throughout the region. In the Philippines, the almost immediate accession to full independence at the war's end was followed by the outbreak of a communist-led rural insurgency known as the Hukbalahap or Huk rebellion. ('Hukbalahap' is a shortened version of the Tagalog words meaning 'People's Army against the Japanese'.)

Building on their record as a guerrilla group that fought against the Japanese, the Huks enjoyed considerable support in the central and southern areas of Luzon where they campaigned for radical change to the land ownership system. Essentially, they called for change that would abolish the large estates and give land to the poor peasantry. This program ran totally contrary to the values and interests of the Philippine elite. When seven Huk candidates were successful in elections held in 1946, the major political parties united to bar the Huks from taking their seats in the Philippines Congress. This decision signalled the beginning of the Huks turning to rebellion against the government in Manila.

Initially, the Huks were successful in setting up an alternative administration in parts of rural Luzon and their leaders spoke of the possibility of their movement becoming national in character. This never happened, for the entrenched political and economic system that linked landowners with tenant farmers and peasants proved to be more powerful than the Huks' calls for dramatic revolutionary change. Nevertheless, between 1946 and 1950, the Huks steadily expanded their control over their Luzon heartland with the Manila government apparently unable to counter their appeal. But by the end of 1950, the Huks were on the defensive and by 1953 they had become little more than a police problem. This rapid reversal of their fortunes began with the capture of their politburo (political leadership) in Manila as the result of a tip to the government from an informer. Coupled with this blow was the energetic leadership shown by Ramon Magsaysay, first as Secretary of Defence and then as President of the Philippines. With considerable assistance from the United States, Magsaysay inspired his troops and called for land reform to undercut the policies that had won support for the Huks among the rural poor.

When Magsaysay died in a plane crash in 1957, the Huks were well and truly defeated, but causes for rural discontent had not disappeared and were to emerge again during the later presidency of Ferdinand Marcos as the base for a new communist-led challenge to the national government in Manila.

Malaya

Just as memories of the Huk rebellion have faded from the minds of outsiders to the Southeast Asian region, so too have memories of the Malayan Emergency, which lasted from 1948 to 1960, been dimmed by the more dramatic events of the Vietnam War and the tragedies of the later Pol Pot period in Cambodia. Although the cost in lives during the Malayan Emergency was small by comparison with the revolutions in Indonesia and Vietnam, its economic costs were considerable. Politically, too, the Emergency was important for the way in which it made clear that the ethnic

Chinese population in Malaya had to make a choice as to where their loyalties lay—whether to a distant Chinese ancestral homeland or to Malaya itself.

Although the Malayan Emergency involved a group of communists mounting an armed challenge to a colonial government, as had happened in Vietnam, there was a fundamental difference between the two situations. In Vietnam it was a case of Vietnamese seeking to gain power. In Malaya what was involved was a case of ethnic Chinese communists, a minority of a minority ethnic group, claiming to act on behalf of the 'Malayan people'. Not only did they have virtually no support for their actions among the majority Malay population, they were denounced by the established leadership of their own ethnic group.

Yet despite the weakness of the insurgents—the total number of active communist guerrillas never exceeded 9000—achieving military victory over them was a long and costly business. Central to the success of the colonial government and the Malayan leadership moving towards independence, was the relocation of Chinese squatter communities to ensure that no aid could be given to the guerrillas, either willingly or under duress. By 1954, the tide had turned against the guerrillas and independence for Malaya was in sight, finally coming in 1957.

There is no doubt that the Emergency delayed the achievement of independence for Malaya, but other factors played their part. Most importantly, it was necessary to find a political formula that took into account the expectation of the Malay community that they would have political dominance in a society that included a very large minority of non-Malays, most particularly ethnic Chinese.

Different countries, different stories

In the four countries discussed in this chapter, the years after the Second World War were marked by violence. But the nature of the violence, the issues for which men fought and died, and the final outcomes were very different. The Indonesian nationalist revolution against Dutch attempts to try and reimpose colonial control was not led by communists, while the Vietnamese force fighting against the French had communists at its head. And the partial success of those Vietnamese communists in 1954 had no parallel elsewhere in Southeast Asia.

The unsuccessful communist revolts in the Philippines and Malaya demonstrated the failure of groups that pursued their goals through violence but which could not make an appeal beyond a limited group within the national population. So revolution and revolt have been a very significant feature of the history of much of Southeast Asia since the Second World War but for very different reasons, in different countries, and at different times.

Other paths to independence

10

Other paths to independence

The conflicts that took place in Indonesia, Vietnam, the Philippines and Malaya emphasise the diverse character of the Southeast Asian region. This chapter is a review of how independence was achieved by the other countries of the region in the decade following the end of the Second World War. Here we are dealing with Burma, Cambodia and Laos. Thailand, of course, was never a colony, and Singapore and the British territories in Borneo did not gain independence until 1963 when they ended their colonial connection by joining Malaysia. Brunei remained a British protectorate until 1984, while the Portuguese only finally abandoned East Timor in 1974.

Burma

When the Second World War ended there was no doubt that Burma would be granted independence by the British, but this did not mean there was an easy transition to the country's new status. The majority ethnic Burmans were split into many rival political groups, while there were long-established rivalries between the Burmans and the other ethnic groups that made up the Burmese population—the Shans, Karens, Chins and Kachins, to mention only the most prominent.

Under British rule there had been special arrangements that meant many of Burma's minorities were governed separately from the majority Burmans. With independence in sight, politicians representing sections of the minority peoples tried to ensure that they would continue to enjoy special rights as they had done under the British. The most able Burmese politician in this immediate post-war period, General Aung San, seemed ready to take account of the interests of the minorities but he and six of his associates were assassinated by political rivals in July 1947. His place was taken by U Nu, the man who was to become the first prime minister of independent Burma and the dominant figure in Burmese politics throughout the 1950s.

Yet although progress towards independence was maintained, it took place in an atmosphere of increasing disunity and rising violence. When independence was proclaimed in January 1948, it was a prelude to a period of grave instability. Finally a full-scale rebellion was launched against the central government by several of the political and minority groups who were unready to accept the country's new political structure. This difficult period foreshadowed Burma's later modern history, which has been marked by political disunity and continuing problems in relations between a government dominated by Burmans and the various ethnic minority elements in the population.

Laos and Cambodia

In contrast with the countries already discussed, the history of developments in Cambodia and Laos in the period after the

Second World War has received limited attention. Yet the terrible tragedies that later occurred in Cambodia and the final emergence of Laos as a communist state can only be understood in terms of what happened in these two countries after 1945.

The contrast between the history of Vietnam and of the other two components of French Indochina, Cambodia and Laos, could not be sharper. While the Vietnamese communists became a vital if almost constantly persecuted force in the 1930s, the same period in Laos and Cambodia saw virtually no agitation along nationalist, let alone communist, lines against the colonial administration. Then, after the French returned to their colonies, nothing took place in Cambodia and Laos to match the armed challenge to the French that developed in Vietnam.

Despite this contrast and the apparent comic opera world of royal courts, sacred elephants, ancient temples and orange-robed monks to be found in both Laos and Cambodia, the Second World War had brought great changes to these countries too.

Laos

In Laos, an anti-French group had emerged during the war years with a royal prince of radical persuasion, Souphanouvong, as one of its most prominent members. When the war ended in 1945, a small group including Souphanouvong refused to embrace the option accepted by other wartime companions. Rather than agree to the return of the French and wait for the eventual granting of self-government and finally independence, Souphanouvong and those sharing his views went into the jungle and linked their goal of independence to the struggle that the neighbouring Vietnamese were just beginning.

Did this mean that the Lao communists did not have a separate identity from their Vietnamese allies? The best answer is 'no', that the communist movement in Laos was, and is, first and foremost a Lao movement. But because of Laos's small population and geographical position, the Lao communists have always been dependent on their ideological allies in Vietnam. During the First Indochina War (the war against the French), areas of northeastern Laos were strategically important to the Vietnamese communists. When threatened by larger French forces, the Vietnamese communist troops could withdraw into Laos. At the same time, the Lao communist forces, the Pathet Lao as they called themselves, worked in close conjunction with, and sometimes under the direction of, the Vietnamese to undermine French control in Laos.

With Vietnam their principal concern, the French worked to maintain political calm in Laos. In this aim they were aided by the general inclination of the Lao elite, a tiny proportion of the total population of three million, to accept the continuing colonial presence. The royal family and the traditional officials were happy, for the most part, to cooperate in a system that brought them personal rewards with a minimum of effort. Prince Souphanouvong with his political commitment, his knowledge of the West gained through education in France, and his readiness to accept the rigours of life in the jungle seemed very much the exception to the general rule.

Following its military defeat at Dien Bien Phu, the French government that negotiated for withdrawal from Vietnam at the Geneva Conference in 1954 no longer had any interest in maintaining control over the weak Kingdom of Laos, which, in any event, had been theoretically independent since 1953. But there was a problem for the French. They wished to transfer power to those conservative Lao who had cooperated with them between 1945 and 1954—the members of the traditional elite. Yet neither the French nor the traditional elite controlled the northern sections of the kingdom in which the communist Pathet Lao were the strongest political and military force. A compromise was finally reached that saw independent Laos agreeing to integrate the Pathet Lao's troops into the country's army.

The compromise failed to work in reality. The independence Laos gained in 1953–54 was flawed from the beginning. The conservative groups in the government had little interest in permitting the left-wing Pathet Lao to gain a legal foothold, while the Pathet Lao were unwilling to be subordinates of their enemies. As had happened between 1945 and 1954, the next chapter in Lao political history was determined, essentially, by developments linked to the Second Indochina War (the Vietnam War).

Cambodia

Unlike Laos, Cambodia did not form a major strategic element in the First Indochina War. Nor did a clearly defined Cambodian communist movement emerge between 1945 and 1953, the date Cambodia officially became independent. Instead, the essential political controversies of those years related to whether Cambodia would be ruled by its hereditary monarch, King Norodom Sihanouk, or governed by equally conservative politicians who wanted the king to be a constitutional monarch without real power. In this contest Sihanouk was the winner. As he grew to political maturity and demonstrated a shrewd capacity to outwit his opponents, he rallied conservative support to his side. As Sihanouk was able to demonstrate his dominance in domestic affairs, he was also able to persuade the French to grant independence to his country in 1953 at a time when the deteriorating situation in Vietnam made resistance to Cambodian demands for an end to the colonial relationship scarcely worthwhile.

During the period of the First Indochina War, and despite the terrible events that later engulfed Cambodia, there was no communist movement of major importance in the country between the end of the Second World War and the granting of independence. There were Vietnamese communist units that used Cambodia for a base and a limited number of Cambodians associated with them, but it would be quite wrong to suggest that in the years between 1946 and 1953 there was a clear communist alternative to Sihanouk and his conservative allies.

What is beyond argument is the fact that Sihanouk came to be regarded by most of his compatriots as the leader who should

Norodom Sihanouk of Cambodia has been one of the most remarkable of Southeast Asia's leaders. Crowned King in 1941, he led his country to independence in 1953. He abdicated his throne in 1955 and was overthrown by close associates in 1970. A prisoner of the Khmer Rouge under Pol Pot, he was again installed as King of Cambodia in 1993.
(PHOTOGRAPH BY DAVID JENKINS COURTESY OF *FAR EASTERN ECONOMIC REVIEW*)

be identified with Cambodia's achievement of independence. As such, he went on to dominate Cambodian politics for more than a decade. Yet this triumph contained the seeds of Cambodia's ultimate disaster.

Independence achieved

By the late 1950s, almost all of Southeast Asia was independent. Thailand had never known formal colonialism. The Philippines had gained independence from the United States at the end of the Second World War, while Burma's path to independence, achieved in 1948, always seemed assured despite internal political squabbling and often-difficult relations with Britain, the departing colonial power. Indonesia's revolution had brought the departure of the Dutch by the end of 1949. And the French had departed from all of the countries of Indochina by the end of 1954, leaving two rival Vietnamese states and Laos and Cambodia.

Britain's colonial links with Malaya were not broken until 1957, in part because of the lingering problems of a communist insurgency. Another factor was the difficulty in finding a political formula that would reconcile the interests of the Malay population, which expected to exercise political dominance, with the interests of the large minority of non-Malay (mostly Chinese) citizens of the country. With a formula finally achieved that assured Malay political dominance but permitted the ethnic Chinese to play a part in the political process, the granting of independence to Malaya left only a residue of British colonial rule in Southeast Asia. Singapore and the territories of Sarawak and North Borneo (now Sabah), were all that remained of Britain's once extensive empire in Southeast Asia. The remaining territories were shortly to end their colonial status when, in 1963, the Federation of Malaysia came into being, uniting independent Malaya with Singapore, Sarawak and Sabah.

Brunei and East Timor: Independence delayed

With the establishment of Malaysia, only Brunei and Portuguese Timor (East Timor) remained as non-independent states in Southeast Asia. The last territory to have remained under Dutch control following Indonesia's gaining independence, Dutch New Guinea, was incorporated into Indonesia in 1963 in controversial circumstances. Brunei remained as a British protectorate. Oil-rich

Brunei was offered the opportunity to join the new Federation of Malaysia, but declined. The Sultan of Brunei feared that his small state's identity would be lost if it became part of Malaysia and that the oil revenues that made Brunei the wealthiest in Southeast Asia would be largely absorbed by the new federation. It was not until January 1984 that Brunei finally assumed a fully independent status.

As for Portuguese Timor, it remained a neglected remnant of Portugal's far-flung colonial empire. Abandoned by its Portuguese rulers as domestic events in Portugal itself led to the collapse of the overseas empire, East Timor was invaded by Indonesia in 1975 and incorporated into that country the following year. Not until 1999, and following a prolonged and bitter guerrilla war, was it possible for East Timor's population to vote in favour of independence following a period of administration by the United Nations.

Facing an independent future

For most, and possibly all, of the former colonies in Southeast Asia, gaining independence brought a sense of relief, and in some cases, great happiness. Even in the war-ravaged circumstances of Vietnam, where the victorious communists only gained control of half the country, there was relief that the fighting had ended and an expectation that control over the whole of Vietnam would not be long delayed. Relief and happiness were natural and readily understood emotions for those who now enjoyed independence. But with that goal achieved, the problems as well as the rewards and pleasures of independence now had to be faced. In many cases, these problems were much greater than the nationalists who had worked to achieve independence, whether through battle or negotiation, had ever expected.

PART III

Independent
Southeast Asia

11

Challenges of the
post-colonial era

For all of the peoples of Southeast Asia, with, as always, the exception of Thailand, attaining independence involved more than a simple change of political control. This change was of basic importance, but more was involved. For many, possibly for most, of the nationalist leaders and their followers there was a sense that in achieving independence they had accomplished something that was almost magical and certainly spiritual in quality. Independence was seen as involving change of all kinds—political, economic and social. But the history of independent Southeast Asia has frequently seen countries of the region having to adjust their programs for change and progress, progress that seemed so readily achievable, as the colonial powers departed.

Seen from the early 21st century, from the perspective of up to fifty years of independence—and with Thailand's experience revealing a very similar pattern of development despite its lack of a colonial past—it is clear that all of the countries of Southeast Asia face major problems. The bright hopes that were so widely held at the time of each country's gaining independence have frequently faded with the passage of time.

The elusive goal of national unity

Achieving and maintaining national unity has been a problem at two main levels throughout Southeast Asia. At one level, there is the problem of finding an agreed form of national government; this is a basic issue about which groups in the community hold power and under what conditions. At the other level, there is the problems of reconciling the interests of regions and minorities.

This second kind of problem—concerned with the clash of interests between the majority group and the minority, or minorities, in the population, or between a central power and a region—can be readily understood by outsiders looking at Southeast Asia. Many examples of conflict and tension between centre of government and region exist elsewhere in the world. The Basque region in Spain is such a case, as are a number of examples in the former Yugoslavia. And even in Britain, that remarkably stable democracy, acknowledgment has been given to the different identities of Scotland and Wales and their interests that sometimes conflict with those of the national government in London.

Achieving national unity has been a problem, to a greater or lesser extent, for all the countries of the region and has led to changes to, or even the complete abandonment of, the political settlements put in place at the time of independence.

Communism in Vietnam, Laos and Cambodia

One of the most important challenges that has faced the governments of independent Southeast Asia has come from the political left, from communism. Yet only in three countries, Vietnam, Laos and Cambodia, have communist governments come to power. Why should this have been so?

There is not much difficulty in offering answers in relation to Vietnam, but providing fully satisfactory answers in relation to Cambodia and Laos presents more of a problem. For Cambodia, most particularly, there are still important gaps in our knowledge of how Pol Pot's Khmer Rouge regime came to power, and these are only slowly being filled. One general point does seem clear: the historical experience of these three countries from the mid-1950s onwards has been very different from that of the other countries of Southeast Asia.

Vietnam

The ultimate success of the Vietnamese communists in establishing a government over the whole of Vietnam reflected a long history of struggle and organisation. Of all the groups that opposed French colonial rule, only the communists were able both to survive French repression and to show that they had a political program that addressed Vietnam's colonial situation. By the end of the Second World War, the communists had become the dominant Vietnamese political group opposing the French. The experience of the First Indochina War reinforced that position. The American attempt to develop a rival Vietnamese state in southern Vietnam after 1954 did not take account of the fact that, however much material aid, and later, massive military assistance, was provided, there was no political movement in Vietnam in the 1950s, 1960s and 1970s that could successfully compete with the communists politically.

The Vietnamese communists won their final battle by military means, but those military means would never have been successful without the unified political direction that existed in the north. Without question, the northern government was ready to exercise harsh control over its own citizens, but there is no denying that it was able to unite them in its war effort. In contrast, non-communist politics in southern Vietnam were marked by squabbles between special interest groups and a lack of ability to forge a sense of national purpose.

This sense of national purpose did not vanish with the end of the war. But peace brought a new set of problems for the communist leaders of united Vietnam. The end of the war revealed that a country so long organised for war was ill-prepared to manage peace. The costs of the long separation of the south from the north brought their own problems, shown most starkly and tragically in the flood of refugees seeking to escape from a society in which they felt they had no place. Vietnam's communist leaders had said repeatedly that they valued independence above all else, and this they did indeed gain in 1975. Yet in the years immediately after their victory, it sometimes seemed that they had little other than independence to offer their people, as their policies led to a regime of severe austerity. It was not until the late 1980s that the government in Hanoi began to embark on a program of economic liberalisation that has proceeded in fits and starts to the present day. It is a program that still has not been matched by political liberalisation.

Laos

The final success of the communists in Vietnam came only after thirty years of war and more than forty years of political action. Nowhere else in Southeast Asia was there a pattern to match this experience. Events in Laos after the Second World War had a certain parallel, as the communist-led Pathet Lao engaged in a political and military struggle that began with the end of the war in 1945 and continued until the communist victory in Vietnam ensured that there would also be a communist victory in Laos in 1975. This does not mean that what took place in Laos was simply an extension of the Vietnam War, no more and no less. Rather, it is a recognition of the fact that the Lao communists were closely linked to their ideological allies in Vietnam and heavily dependent on them in political and military terms. Moreover, the position Laos occupied during the Vietnam War reflected a long historical continuity. The territory of modern Laos had traditionally been a buffer region between Vietnam and Thailand. In their concern to see a communist victory in Laos, the Vietnamese communists were following what had long been historical policy, that of making sure that no other hostile state could play a significant role in Laos, and in particular in those regions of Laos close to its border with Vietnam.

Cambodia

If events leading to a final communist victory in Laos may be seen, in some senses, as a footnote to what happened in Vietnam, the same is most certainly not the case for Cambodia. The problem for that country is how to explain the dramatic shift from a country ruled by a king in the 1950s to the seizure of power by an ultra-radical left-wing group in the mid-1970s.

To many outsiders, it appeared that Prince Norodom Sihanouk in the 1950s and 1960s had successfully found a formula for governing Cambodia that guaranteed his control of domestic politics while pursuing a foreign policy that preserved Cambodia's neutrality. Hindsight makes clear that much of this success was an illusion. Domestically, there was no place in Sihanouk's Cambodia for those who disagreed with his policies. For those who had embraced left-wing views, there were only two alternatives: either they could remain silent or they could slip into the countryside to join the small but growing band of those who were waiting for a time when it might be possible to attempt a seizure of power. In the event, the challenge that removed Sihanouk from power came not from the leftists who had joined the communist cause but from right-wing politicians. In overthrowing Sihanouk, they set the stage for one of the bitterest struggles by a left-wing group to gain power in all the recent history of Southeast Asia.

The coup by the men of the right was followed by Cambodia's involvement in the Vietnam War, as the United States tried to buy time for the withdrawal of its forces from Vietnam. After America invaded Cambodia in 1970 in an effort to strike at Vietnamese communist bases there, the Vietnamese communists responded by lending their support to the Cambodian communists fighting against the government in Phnom Penh. As the Cambodian communist forces became stronger, the Vietnamese scaled down their level of assistance. By the end of 1972, the war had settled into a bloody pattern in which the Phnom Penh government forces—with massive American assistance, including bombing strikes of unparalleled intensity—faced a much smaller but remarkably determined left-wing enemy. If numbers and massive military assistance could win wars, then the Phnom Penh regime should have won. That it did not do so reflects the remarkable determination of the left-wing forces and the poor leadership displayed by the Phnom Penh regime.

As the war continued, it became clear that widespread brutality was the norm and not the exception. Perhaps the left-wing forces saw the use of harshly violent tactics against civilians as well as soldiers as a necessary weapon for a numerically weaker side. Possibly, too, their use of violence was not only a strategy to match the violence of the Phnom Penh forces but also a reaction to the ferocity of the bombing by United States aircraft. Whatever the reasons, the level of political violence and of atrocities committed by both sides increased as the war continued. For the left-wing leadership, the experience of these years reinforced their conviction that if they were victorious, there would be no place for half-measures in the way in which they would govern. Cambodia was to be transformed completely, no matter what the cost in human lives and suffering.

Total transformation was what the Khmer Rouge (Red Khmer or Cambodians) worked for after their victory in April 1975. Led

Mass graves throughout Cambodia are a ghastly legacy of the Pol Pot period of misrule over Cambodia. Following the Vietnamese invasion of Cambodia in late 1978, many of these graves have been exhumed and the skulls of Pol Pot's victims have been grouped by the graves as a reminder of the hundreds of thousands who died by execution between 1975 and 1979. The skulls and bones in this photograph were at a grave close to Phnom Penh that was being exhumed in late 1981.

by Pol Pot, the government of Democratic Kampuchea pursued policies that they claimed were necessary to remove the corrupt influences of foreign and capitalist societies and to achieve their goal of making Cambodia agriculturally self-sufficient. The outside world only slowly came to learn of the means by which these goals were to be achieved, for after the Khmer Rouge victory, Cambodia was almost completely closed to foreign visitors. Nevertheless, it slowly became clear that Pol Pot and his associates were using shocking methods to achieve their ends. These began with the mass forced evacuation of Phnom Penh in circumstances that involved great cruelty and suffering. The bulk of the Cambodian population was herded into vast agricultural cooperatives. There they were expected to work in inhuman conditions, risking sudden punishment, including execution, for even a minor failure to follow the harsh rules that governed their lives.

The cost in human lives of this period of tyranny under Pol Pot was staggering. It will never be clear how many Cambodians were executed between 1975 and 1979, nor is it possible to be absolutely certain as to how many persons lost their lives as a result of the terrible conditions under which the Cambodian population was forced to live. Today, the best estimate is that no less than two million Cambodians died as a result of policies followed by Pol Pot's government. Of that two million, possibly as many as 500 000 were executed.

We cannot judge how long Pol Pot and his associates might have continued their bloody rule if Vietnam had not invaded Cambodia at the end of 1978, ousting the Khmer Rouge regime from Phnom Penh in January 1979. The possibility is that Pol Pot's government might have continued on its horrific course for some time. But once the Khmer Rouge decided to mount cross-border raids into southern Vietnam, they were signing their regime's death warrant. Much stronger than the Cambodian military forces, the Vietnamese rapidly overcame Khmer Rouge resistance and put in place a new government in Phnom Penh made up of Cambodians favourable to Hanoi.

This was not the end to conflict in Cambodia. At one level, Vietnam's invasion delivered the Cambodian population from a terrible tyranny. But in doing so the Vietnamese created a situation that China and the members of ASEAN (the Association of Southeast Asian Nations, composed at this time of Indonesia, Malaysia, the Philippines, Singapore and Thailand) were not prepared to accept. Cambodia became an element in the continuing Cold War and it was not until the Cold War ended following the collapse of the Soviet Union at the end of the 1980s that it was possible for a solution to be found to the continuing hostilities in Cambodia. With the United Nations playing a major role in bringing a new administration into being, democratic elections were held in Cambodia in 1992. These were, without doubt, the freest and fairest elections ever to be held in Cambodia.

Balancing the present and the past

For all the countries of Southeast Asia the modern period has been a time when it has been necessary to try and strike a balance between the demands of the present and the values of the past. With the end of colonial control, Southeast Asians have, for the most part, been able to make their own decisions and to judge how much they should rely on their own values and the lessons they draw from history. The results of this situation have not always been what Southeast Asians, let alone outsiders, have expected for, in various ways, the post-colonial settlements in the countries of the region have come under examination and strain. The consequences have sometimes been dramatic and are looked at in the next chapter.

12

Contemporary Southeast Asia

If we sometimes feel overwhelmed by the complicated nature of Southeast Asia's past, the same comment often seems just as true when looking at is present. There are major differences from country to country, in terms of their political systems, their economies and the extent to which tradition lives on in company with the new. Life in the cities is very different from life in the provinces. And in the rural regions there are enormous contrasts between the lives of those who farm in areas favoured by good climate and soils and others who scrape a bare living in regions deprived of both these benefits.

It is certainly not possible to sum up Southeast Asia's long history in a single phrase or sentence for, as the previous chapters have made clear, the region's history has been full of events that have been the result of particular circumstances in individual countries. So while it is possible to point to general patterns across Southeast Asia, the existence of these patterns always has to be

Despite the impact of modernity in Southeast Asia, old methods of transport still play a part in the region's cities, as seen here in the example of an ox cart in Cambodia's capital, Phnom Penh, and a bicycle rickshaw or cyclopousse *in Vietnam's largest southern city, Saigon.*

balanced against the individual and sometimes unique character of developments in one country or another.

Modern Southeast Asia still has the capacity to surprise and in doing so, to alert an outsider to the error of thinking that it is simply a region becoming part of a modern world in which Western styles of building, of dressing and of eating are the dominant models. The towering skyline in central Jakarta or McDonald's restaurant on Singapore's Orchard Road, the Makati business district in Manila or Bangkok's tourist strip along Sukhumvit Road—all these suggest that Southeast Asia is moving towards some kind of global standard of living and behaviour.

Such a view is badly misleading. A random event can still bring this home to a visitor to the region. Move away from the tall buildings on Jalan Thamrin, one of Jakarta's main thoroughfares, and walk through the back lanes of this sprawling city. A visitor who does this might well hear a Balinese *gamelan* orchestra at practice. Having come to Indonesia's capital in search of jobs, the members of this orchestra are playing the same melodies they would perform on their home island, only here they play their xylophones and gongs in a dusty inner urban space rather than in the elegant surroundings of a temple in Bali.

Every year, festivals large and small take place throughout Southeast Asia and these are links to the past as well as causes for celebrating the present. The further a visitor travels away from the main cities of the region, the more it becomes clear that the impact of the modern world is often very much a surface affair. And it is certainly the case that in the rural areas of Southeast Asia, traditional patterns of leadership and authority remain very important at the level of the village.

New leaders, old traditions

In presenting a balanced view of the various aspects of Southeast Asia—old and new, modern and traditional—the emphasis throughout this book has been on the need to take account of both continuity and change. Nowhere have these two elements been more obvious than in the kind of leaders who emerged in many Southeast Asian countries in the years immediately after independence. Cambodia provides the clearest example of a post-independence leader who played a role that was closely linked to the position traditionally occupied by a king. As king, prime minister and, later, chief of state, Norodom Sihanouk gained great political benefit from his royal status and behaved with a regal conviction that his political judgments were not open to question. This conviction in the absolute rightness of his view played a major part in the decision of his right-wing enemies to depose him in 1970.

In a very different political setting, and despite his lack of royal ancestors, Sukarno, as the first president of Indonesia, assumed many of the characteristics of a traditional Javanese ruler. And for a period he was admired by his compatriots for behaving in this fashion, even though this meant that Sukarno became increasingly reckless and autocratic in both his domestic and international policies. Ultimately he became so assured of his own rightness, and of his political invulnerability, that he failed to recognise that he had lost the support of the Indonesian military who were vital to his retaining power. When, after a failed coup in 1965, the military turned against him, Sukarno's hold on the Indonesian presidency was doomed.

Other examples of the continuing importance of traditional leadership reinforce the point. The first Prime Minister of Malaya (later Malaysia), Tunku Abdul Rahman, was a Malay prince, and his immediate successors were Malay aristocrats. Even in the case of communist Vietnam and Laos, it is possible to see clear links with the traditional view of leadership in the persons of Ho Chi Minh and Prince Souphanouvong. In his personal austerity and his mastery of many languages, not least the classical Chinese in which he wrote his poems, Ho Chi Minh fitted well with the long-established Vietnamese ideal of a scholar. This in no way

Tunku Abdul Rahman was the 'father' of Malaysia's independence and its country's first prime minister. Born a prince, he became an active politician during the Second World War. During the period of the Malayan Emergency Tunku Abdul Rahman exemplified the commitment of Malay politicians to work with the British to defeat the Communist insurgents while preparing for independence. (PHOTOGRAPH COURTESY OF FAR EASTERN ECONOMIC REVIEW)

prevented his being honoured at the same time for the nationalist goals he pursued through his long-time commitment to communism. Prince Souphanouvong never ceased to behave like a Lao aristocrat as he devoted his life to left-wing causes. Confirming the importance of the part played by the traditional elite once Laos gained independence, Souphanouvong's half-brother, Prince Souvanna Phouma, led the party that tried to achieve a neutralist solution to Laos's political and military conflicts. And yet another Prince, Boun Oum, briefly played a prominent role in Laos's political life in the 1960s.

Yet in pointing to these examples of the continuing importance of royalty and other traditional values there is a risk of failing to notice the much more important changes that have taken place in the leadership and administrations that now exist throughout the region. Two hundred years ago, all of the major states of Southeast Asia were headed by kings or other hereditary rulers. At the beginning of the twenty-first century a hereditary ruler is the chief of state in only three countries: Brunei, Cambodia and Thailand. And in only one, Brunei, does the ruler exercise power in an unqualified fashion. The chief of state of Malaysia is also a king, but this is an elective office with no real power. What has occurred over the nineteenth and twentieth centuries has been the disappearance of traditional royal rulers and systems of government linked to the rulers' courts. In their place, new administrative systems have come into being and these have been largely based on Western models.

Increasingly, leadership in Southeast Asia is either in the hands of politicians who fit into a general Westernised intellectual mould, or who are served by advisers who have these characteristics. For all its emphasis on Maraxist–Leninist ideology, Vietnam, the most important communist state in Southeast Asia, falls into this pattern. Vietnam's leaders have had a rather special exposure to Western influence, but Marxist thought must be reckoned a Western product even though it sits alongside other traditional influences in Vietnam, including those adopted from China. Of course, there is room for all kinds of qualifications. Above all, it is important to recognise that change from traditional to more modern forms of administration has taken place at different speeds in different countries. Singapore's adoption of Western forms of adminis-tration, while seeking to draw on traditional values such as those associated with the importance of the family, certainly stands in contrast to the reclusive values of Burma's military-dominated regime. Yet for all the emphasis of successive Burmese leaders on the need to follow a Burmese route to socialism, that country's leaders have administered the state through an administrative system inherited from the British colonial power.

Cambodia under the Pol Pot tyranny was an exception to the general pattern just described. For more than three years, between 1975 and 1979, Cambodia's leaders turned their back on the form of administration that the country had inherited from the French. As noted in the previous chapter, why they adopted such a radical new system is still being debated. Two factors were certainly involved. Pol Pot and his associates believed that Sihanouk's regime and its successor, after Sihanouk was deposed in 1970, were utterly corrupt, so there had to be a total break with the past. In addition, the terrible civil war fought in Cambodia between 1970 and 1975 hardened their determination to totally remake society. But with their limited understanding of communist theory and their unrealistic wish to make Cambodia totally self-sufficient agriculturally, they presided over a tyrannical system of government that cost the lives of upwards of two million persons. And this tragedy unfolded as the Pol Pot regime embarked on an aggressive policy of armed attacks against Vietnam, ultimately leading to a Vietnamese response that toppled the Khmer Rouge regime in 1979.

Pol Pot's determination to attack Vietnam with the proclaimed purpose of regaining Cambodian territory lost to Vietnam centuries before defies rational explanation, particularly given the fact that Cambodia's military forces were so inferior in number to Vietnam's. A tone of paranoia is present in the Khmer Rouge's justification for their actions, published only months before the Vietnamese invasion brought the end to Pol Pot's rule.

Thus, whether it is during the life of the feudalists, of the French colonialists, of the American imperialists, or of Ho Chi Minh (that is to say, in the contemporary period), the Vietnamese have not changed their nature of being an aggressor, an annexationist, and a swallower of the territory of other countries.

(LIVRE NOIR, *BLACK BOOK*, 1978)

The terrible case of Cambodia aside, the twentieth century saw the rise to importance throughout Southeast Asia of technocrats, men and women whose skills ensured them a place in the government of their country. In some cases, these 'new men' and 'new women' dominate the political system. At other times they work in uneasy balance with traditional leaders. Only in special cases can they be ignored.

They are not only 'new' in terms of their training. Although many of those who have risen to power since the Second World War have been members of the region's traditional elite, this is not always the case. To some extent, what has taken place has been

Lee Kuan Yew has dominated Singapore's politics since 1959, and continues to do so despite stepping down from the position of prime minister. A brilliant British-trained lawyer, he has presided over Singapore's extraordinary transformation from a colonial entrepôt into a thriving modern city. (PHOTOGRAPH BY S.T. TAN COURTESY OF FAR EASTERN ECONOMIC REVIEW)

the replacement of one form of elite (the traditional) with another (the elite of merit). Changed political conditions and improved educational opportunities have not always guaranteed the success of talent in modern Southeast Asia, but the barriers are now a great deal lower than they once were. Most particularly is this so in Singapore, where the long-serving prime minister, Lee Kuan Yew, made intellectual ability the key qualification for advancement in Singapore's administration. This policy has continued under his successor.

Administrative changes and the increasing importance of 'new' men and women in Southeast Asia has not meant that Western-style democracy was adopted throughout the region. Far from it, as the case of the communist states of Laos and Vietnam have shown. The case of Indonesia is equally instructive. When former President Suharto came to power in the late 1960s, the Indonesian government embraced economic policies drawn up by advisers who had close links with the free market theories promoted by the economic faculties of major American universities. Yet the pursuit of modern economic policies did not mean that the Suharto regime was ready to run Indonesia under any system that was based on a version of Western democracy. It was only with the fall of Suharto's regime in 1998 that major change took place, finally leading to Indonesia's having a president elected through a democratic process.

The end of flexible boundaries

Territorial disputes make headlines, as do separatist claims from regions such as Aceh and Irian Jaya (Papua) in Indonesia. But the attention given to such matters disguises the fact that, overall, the countries of contemporary Southeast Asia exist within territorial boundaries that are mostly fixed and unchallenged. In the light of history, this is a remarkable state of affairs, not least because several of the states of modern Southeast Asia only achieved their present territorial existence in very recent times. Modern-day Laos was a cluster of principalities and even smaller petty states when the French imposed colonial control at the end of the nineteenth century. The Federation of Malaysia is made up of sultanates that had no shared unity a century ago, as well as territories in Borneo that were disputed by two sultanates and areas in the interior of that great island that lay quite outside the maritime Islamic sultans' world. Indonesia was forged from the colonial empire of the Dutch East Indies, which in turn only achieved overall control of the islands it claimed to govern at the beginning of the twentieth century. The Spaniards regarded the Philippines as a single political unit, but they never successfully administered all of the territories they claimed.

So, one distinctive feature of modern Southeast Asia's history has been the extent to which, over the past hundred years, the old, loose boundaries and administrative arrangements have become tighter, confirming the existence of old states, such as Burma and Vietnam, and defining the territorial existence of new ones. Indonesia, Malaysia and Laos are modern creations, whatever long historical traditions may be appealed to in order to show that these modern states had important predecessors. Southeast Asia's modern history, both in colonial times and after independence, has confirmed the boundaries of Burma, Cambodia, Thailand and Vietnam, and given emphasis to the existence of the Philippines as a single political unit. Singapore is a creation of the nineteenth and twentieth centuries, and a state that might be seen, perhaps a little romantically, as a descendant of another, long ago entrepôt, Srivijaya.

East Timor: A special case

East Timor has to be written about as a special case, the exception to the general rule that the identities inherited by the newly independent states of Southeast Asia after the Second World War followed on from those established at the end of colonial control. A long-neglected part of Portugal's ramshackle colonial empire, East Timor was considered a potential threat to the stability of Suharto's Indonesia when the Portuguese administration abandoned the territory in the mid-1970s. Indonesia's invasion of East Timor in 1975 and its incorporation into Indonesia in 1976 seemed to many observers to spell the end to any possibility that the territory could gain independence in its own right. That it finally did so is a reflection of many things. Indonesian brutality and incompetence fuelled local resistance and saw the emergence of a determined group of guerrillas who were ready to fight for independence. By the time of the collapse of the Suharto regime at the end of the 1990s, Indonesian opinion was divided about the worth of trying to retain control over East Timor. And, importantly, there was long-running opposition to Indonesia's takeover of East Timor in the international community, both at the level of governments and among their populations.

Having finally achieved independence, East Timor faces a difficult future. Despite the prospect of substantial income from oil and gas resources in the years to come, it will be economically dependent on international aid for many years. Above all, its independent government lacks skilled personnel and will have to find employment for a population that is overwhelmingly youthful. The good feelings generated by the achievement of independence provide little, if any, guarantee of solutions for the problems of this newest of Southeast Asia's states.

Class, economics, ethnicity and religion

Issues linked to class and economics have dominated politics in the countries of the Western world over the past hundred years. Political battles have been fought over how national revenue should be spent, who will benefit from particular policies and how to create future wealth. Yet it's not at all clear that issues such as these have always been central for many of the politicians of modern Southeast Asia. In some cases, economic considerations have clearly taken second place to other concerns. Burma provides a striking example. Although in recent years Burma has taken some limited steps towards opening up its economy to the wider world, for decades it undertook a search for 'the Burmese road to socialism' that restricted contact of all kinds with the outside world. This reflected a judgment by its leaders that maintaining internal control, and in particular maintaining the control of the Burman ethnic majority over the other ethnic groups within the state, was more important than trying to match the economic progress of some of Burma's neighbours.

The policies followed in Burma have some echoes in both Vietnam and Laos. In both these countries, following the communist victories of 1975, the principal concern of the government leadership has been to maintain the unchallenged political position of each country's communist party. By the end of the 1990s, both Vietnam and Laos had allowed some degree of economic liberalisation, but this has always been done with an eye on the possibility that too much relaxation of state control of the economy might lead to the current strict party control of political life coming under threat. Freewheeling commercial enterprise may seem a feature of life in Saigon (Ho Chi Minh City), but this is only permitted so long as there is no suggestion that a large degree of commercial freedom should be matched by accompanying political liberalisation. The parallel with China is striking, so that in Vietnam, and to a lesser extent in Laos, China provides an unacknowledged model of how to separate commerce and politics.

In other countries, and notably in Malaysia, concerns with ethnicity play a major part in politics. There is scarcely a facet of Malaysian life that is not affected by the fact that while Malays are in the majority and are the dominant political group, their leaders worry about the commercial success of the minority

Chinese population. Once again, reference needs to be made to the importance of ethnic politics in Burma, where a large number of ethnic groups often see their interests as different from those of the majority Burmans. And problems arising from the interplay of ethnicity and politics can also exist where the numbers of ethnic minorities are relatively small. Vietnam provides an example. As Vietnam's population increases in size, majority Vietnamese have moved to establish themselves in areas that once were the preserve of minority hill peoples, with clashes resulting between the two groups.

In the Philippines, religion cannot be separated from politics. With a population that is 90 per cent Christian, the 5 per cent of the population which follows Islam is far from fully integrated into the state. Concentrated in the southern islands of the archipelago, Muslim resentment of the essentially Christian government in Manila has led to hostilities that show little likelihood of early solution. Clashes between Muslims and Christians have become a major problem in the Moluccas (Maluku), the eastern Indonesian islands that were once known as the 'Spice Islands'. Here, where for many years communities following different religions lived peacefully side by side, political and economic uncertainty in recent years have contributed to a breakdown in relations. And even where outright hostilities have not been present, as is the case in southern Thailand there is a substantial Islamic minority, the presence of a group with a different religion from that of the majority (Buddhist) community adds a special and difficult character to contemporary politics.

Population, health, environment, education and economy

It would be very wrong to write about the difficulties facing Southeast Asian countries as if the developed countries of the Western world, in contrast, have no problems of their own. Yet a convincing case can be made for the argument that there are major problems in Southeast Asia that are of a different kind from those in the West, not least because the colonial powers had ruled according to different priorities from those of the newly independent regimes that followed them.

Population

The problem of rapid population growth makes the point. In many countries in Western Europe, population growth has slowed to be almost negligible, or has even fallen below replacement level. In other developed countries, such as the United States and Australia, continuing immigration has been an important factor in ensuring population growth.

The contrast with Southeast Asia is striking. The situation is most dramatic in Indonesia, the country in the region with the largest population. In 1950, just after independence, the Indonesian population was calculated to be about 78 million. Fifty years later, in 2000, the size of Indonesia's population had risen to an estimated 210 million, an increase of more than 260 per cent. And although the rate at which Indonesia's population is increasing has now slowed, some estimates are that it will not reach a plateau—the point at which it is no longer increasing—for another forty or fifty years. At that point, the more pessimistic estimates suggest that the population of Indonesia will total upwards of 400 million.

These increases represent enormous challenges for the governments of the region, for larger populations mean a greater drain on the services governments are expected to provide. The provision of basic services, such as the supply of clean drinking water, becomes an ever greater problem as cities expand. Health services and the availability of universal primary education are increasingly expected by more and more people, yet matching resources to demand will become even more difficult than it is today as the numbers making those demands grow.

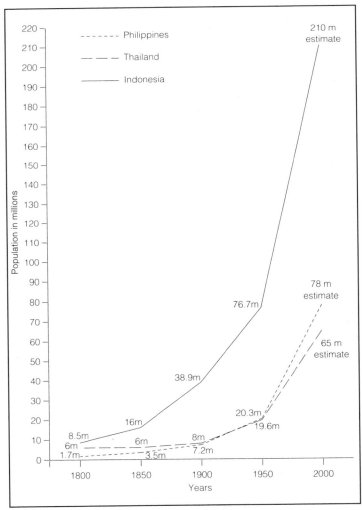

Population growth in Indonesia, the Philippines and Thailand, 1800–2000
*Population growth in Southeast Asia has been dramatic during the twentieth century.
Even with government-supported efforts to limit population growth in Indonesia, that
country's population had already reached an estimated 210 million in the year 2000.*

Health

Of all the health problems that face the governments of Southeast Asia, none is more serious than the HIV-AIDS pandemic. HIV-AIDS has joined the long list of existing major health problems of malaria, tuberculosis, leprosy and dysentery, to pose a terrible threat to the region. Each time figures are cited for the number of sufferers, they need to be adjusted upwards shortly after. In the case of some countries, it is quite clear that official figures bear no relation to the true, and grim, reality. While Thailand has been open in its acknowledgment of the problems and costs that it faces because of HIV-AIDS, other countries have been reluctant to give an accurate account of the scale of the disease within their boundaries. Their reluctance stems from many things, from a lack of reliable statistics to ideological or religious reasons for not publicising the true state of affairs.

Although the scale of the HIV-AIDS pandemic in Southeast Asia has not yet reached the proportions of what has occurred and is continuing to occur in sub-Saharan Africa, there is no doubt that the situation is going to become worse before its effects can be slowed. Before that point is reached, the cost to individual Southeast Asian countries is going to be immense, eating up health budgets and prospectively having a major effect on economic performance. And these costs are over and above the human misery caused by the disease.

The onset of the HIV-AIDS crisis has affected the poor most grievously. It has been the poor and uneducated who are most at risk, a fact that highlights the continuing existence of areas of Southeast Asia where poverty is the norm, not the exception. These are areas where poverty has been present for many decades and even many centuries. Included are upland regions, such as those found in Laos and Cambodia, where hill peoples have long practised slash-and-burn agriculture and live at the margin of existence. But it is not only among such minority groups that poverty is found. The rural population of parts of central and eastern Java have been impoverished since the nineteenth century. Northeastern Thailand is the poorest region in a country that has other areas that are very well-suited to productive agriculture. Some of the central provinces of Vietnam have been home to poverty since before the arrival of the French colonialists.

A distinctive feature of Southeast Asia's history in the twentieth century has been the growth of urban poverty. On the outskirts of most, if not all, the major cities of modern Southeast Asia are slums accommodating the urban poor. Many are first-generation slum-dwellers, former rural peasants who have come to the city in the hope that it will provide more opportunities to gain a livelihood than was possible in the regions where they were born. But many, too, are second- and even third-generation victims of poverty who have found that their families' hopes—that coming to live in the city would open the way to a new and prosperous life—have been sadly disappointed.

Environment

Hand in hand with the problems of health are the concerns associated with threats to the region's environment. Brief reference has already been made to the concerns linked to the supply of clean drinking water for the inhabitants of Southeast Asia's rapidly growing cities. But this is not the only challenge associated with water supply. Increasingly there are worries that there is not enough water for irrigation in many of the region's vitally important rice-growing areas. In other cases, dams have been built that have badly affected fish stocks, while deforestation has added to the destructive rapid run-off of topsoil into rivers and lakes. Most disturbingly of all for the countries of mainland Southeast Asia, and for Cambodia and Vietnam in particular, dams being built on the upper course of the Mekong River in China risk making a fundamental alteration to that river's character. If the existing flow of the Mekong is altered, the consequences for Cambodia's Great Lake and for the Mekong Delta in Vietnam could be very serious. The Great Lake is the source of the fish that supply 60 per cent of the Cambodian population's annual protein intake, while the Mekong Delta is vital to Vietnam both for its rice crops and other agricultural crops as well as for fishing.

Southeast Asia is rapidly losing the forests that once covered the greater part of its territory as trees are felled to make way for agriculture and plantations and to meet the demands of the developed world for hardwood timbers. This is a problem in both mainland and maritime Southeast Asia, and nowhere has this been more striking than in the Philippines. In 1946, there were 30 million hectares of hardwood forests in the Philippines. By 1990 (the latest date available for reliable statistics), the area of hardwood forests had been reduced to less than 1 million hectares. In Vietnam, the cost to the environment as the result of the Vietnam War was the destruction of 2.2 million hectares of forest and farmland. Even more forest has been destroyed since 1975, when the war ended. In the course of post-war reconstruction, Vietnam has been using 200 000 hectares of forest each year. In Cambodia, the country that has suffered more than any other in Southeast Asia in the post-colonial period, the results of illegal logging in the 1990s have been devastating. So much so that, in 1998, the Asian Development Bank warned that if an end was not put to illegal logging, Cambodia's resources of tropical hardwood would be exhausted in five years. Some heed has been taken of this dire warning, but illegal logging continues, if on a reduced scale.

One of the consequences of clearing forests, and the accompanying burning of undergrowth before cleared areas are brought to cultivation, has been the generation of vast clouds of smoke haze. In recent years, clearing and burning, principally in Indonesian Borneo (Kalimatan) and Sumatra, have left a vast smoke haze hanging over wide areas of Southeast Asia, from Singapore and Malaysia to the Philippines. On occasion, the haze has remained in place for more than a month at a time. As a result, there have been widespread health problems as the haze has caused a rise in respiratory illnesses and eye irritations.

Education and economy

Although all of the colonial regimes that ruled in Southeast Asia paid some attention to the need to provide education for at least part of the population they governed, none, not even the most enlightened, promoted a system of universal education, at the primary level on the same basis as they did in their own countries. So, in embracing the aim of universal primary education the newly independent governments had to find new resources, both of money and teachers.

At a different level, the colonial governments of Southeast Asia generally did little to prepare their citizens for the time when they would have to play a direct role in the economic life of the community. With the colonies valued for their economic resources, there was a widespread pattern in which European or American companies controlled major international commerce, while internal commerce was shared between the colonisers and immigrant Asian communities, usually Chinese or Indian. As a result, the leaders of the newly independent states found that they had only limited control over their own economies. The situation had a political aspect to it as well as an economic one. For colonial governments, the immigrant communities played a vital role, particularly in commerce and in providing labour for plantations and public works. In contrast to the independent governments of the region, the immigrant communities represented something different—at best a group posing problems of assimilation, at worst a threat to the security of the state.

An end to post-colonial settlements

The challenges and problems that have just been described have gone hand in hand with major transformations in the political arrangements established in the various states of Southeast Asia and an outline of the changes that have occurred now follows.

The mainland states

Nowhere has this dismantling of earlier political arrangements been more apparent than in the countries of Southeast Asia that were once controlled by France. Vietnam provides the most striking example of this process. In that country, arrangements brought into being at the end of the colonial period came under challenge and were then the cause of a long and costly war. Divided between north and south, and between communism and an authoritarian form of capitalism, the two Vietnamese states that emerged after the departure of the French in 1954 were backed by the then Cold War rivals, the Soviet Union and the United States of America. It was only after twenty-one years of guerrilla skirmishes that turned into full-scale war that Vietnam achieved its present political and territorial unity. Conservative estimates place the number of Vietnamese who died during the Vietnam War at over three million.

Cambodia's post-colonial history has been equally traumatic. When Cambodia achieved independence in 1953, King Norodom Sihanouk appeared the country's unchallengeable leader, a situation apparently reinforced by his abdication in 1955 to take a full-time role in politics. Yet, unrecognised by almost all observers, forces were at work that Sihanouk could not control. Right-wing opponents threw Sihanouk out of office in 1970, only to be defeated in their turn by a radical local communist movement that, temporarily, was aligned with the Vietnamese communists. The terrible years of the Pol Pot tyranny were followed by Vietnam's occupation of Cambodia and the installation of a puppet regime in 1979. Only after another ten years of conflict was it possible for the international community, working through the United Nations, to find a way to bring a shaky peace to Cambodia.

Immediately after achieving independence in 1953, it was clear that Laos had been left with a political system that would not work, for it satisfied neither royalists, nor neutralists, nor communists. So the country suffered through a series of coups and counter-coups. These pitched right-wing and pro-royalist forces against neutralists, while the local communists fought with the single goal of gaining total power. The final victors were the communists who, in 1975, established a one-party state which tolerated no opposition. Since that date there has been no serious challenge to the unity of the Lao state. Nevertheless, a low-level insurgency continues to fester within Laos, and the minority Hmong hill people, who were once associated with American forces during the Vietnam War, mount hit-and-run raids against government troops and isolated outposts.

The other two states of mainland Southeast Asia have made their own adjustments to the patterns of government that existed in the 1940s. In Thailand's case, the changes that have taken place over the past fifty years have not followed the achievement of independence from a colonial power. Nevertheless, events in Thailand have had many similarities with what occurred elsewhere in Southeast Asia. In Thailand, too, there has been a search to find a form of government that could ensure national unity. The past readiness of the country's military to impose its will through coups d'état against the government of the day was a very particular reflection of this search for a stable government that could command popular support.

Often forgotten now, in the light of Thailand's slow but continuing progress towards greater democracy, was the threat posed during the 1970s by an insurgency led by the Communist Party of Thailand (CPT). The CPT was most active in the poor provinces of Thailand's northeast, and for a period there were grave fears that its armed groups might be able to match the successes of the communists in Vietnam, Laos and Cambodia. This did not happen, as the government in Bangkok followed a classic carrot-and-stick approach to overcoming the insurgency. Offers of amnesty and the diversion of funds to improve the lot of poor peasants was accompanied by harsh military operations against those CPT members who continued to try and advance their cause through military means. Today, despite some continuing separatist feeling among Thai followers of Islam in the south, Thailand has achieved a high degree of unity under a much-loved king.

The arrangements put in place at the time Burma gained independence in 1947 never really came to grips with the divided had as one of its dominant characteristics the clash between the efforts of Burmans to impose their control over the non-Burman elements of the population. In the pre-colonial past, the Burmans succeeded in establishing a shaky control over the Shans, Kachins, Karens and other minority groups. Once British colonial rule was removed, the old tensions between the dominant Burmans and other ethnic groups within the state re-emerged and these continue to pose problems more than fifty years after independence.

Furthermore, the parliamentary system was constantly hampered by a large number of parties with conflicting aims, while no satisfactory system was found to deal with the discontented minority groups, many of which were at war with the central government. The ultimate result was that Burma's military seized power and made clear that they were unready to share control of the country with an elected parliament. The situation, with occasional minor modifications, has continued to the present day despite clear evidence that the population at large would welcome a return to representative government. Without radical political change, Burma seems fated to continue as a country in which a government dominated by a military junta rejects calls for democracy and cannot completely eliminate armed opposition from minority ethnic groups. In turn, these ethnic groups are never likely to be strong enough to achieve their goals of enjoying a truly autonomous existence, separate from the Burmans who have been their rivals at best and enemies at worst.

The maritime states

Compared to the political and economic difficulties that have plagued Indonesia and the Philippines since independence, Malaysia's history since the end of colonial rule in 1957 appears remarkably stable. And so, at the broadest level, it has been. Yet Malaysia still faces problems because of its ethnic composition, a fact that led in the early 1970s to a fundamental adjustment to the political arrangements that had been put in place at the time of independence. Stated simply, these arrangements assumed that political power would be in the hands of the Malays, while commercial power would be ceded to Malaysia's large ethnic Chinese population. (The ethnic Indian minority was not sufficiently large to play a determining role in these arrangements.)

As Britain began to make arrangements to withdraw its lingering colonial presence from Singapore and the Borneo territories of Sabah and Sarawak, a decision was made to expand Malaya to become the Federation of Malaysia, by incorporating Singapore and the Borneo territories. The new federation came into being in 1963, but within two years, it became clear that Malaysia's ethnic Malay politicians and Singapore's largely Chinese leaders could not work together, and Singapore was expelled from the federation before the end of 1965.

Four years after this shock, the fact that not all was well within Malaysia became sharply apparent when, in May 1969, large-scale riots in Kuala Lumpur involving Malays and Chinese led to the imposition of a state of emergency. At the heart of these serious disturbances were two unresolved issues. On the one hand, younger Malays were no longer ready to accept that it was enough to hold political power without accompanying economic power. On the other side of the ethnic divide were young Chinese, who could not accept that their political representatives should forever renounce the possibility of gaining political power equal to that held by Malays.

With calm restored, the Malaysian government inaugurated a new political and economic set of constitutional arrangements. Central to these was the 'New Economic Policy'. Under this policy, the government gave preferred status to Malays in a wide range of activities, from the granting of business licences to the opportunity to study at universities. This system of affirmative action has remained in place to the present day. Ethnic Chinese continue to play a major part in Malaysia's business and commerce, and they occupy seats in parliament, but they do so in a system that makes clear that ethnic Malay dominance will be assured in all important aspects of life within the country.

Given its great size and the varied nature of its population spread across so many islands, it should not be surprising that over the past fifty years, Indonesia has found its national unity under challenge on a number of occasions. As a result of these challenges, the political arrangements put in place at the end of the Indonesian revolution in 1948 have changed significantly over the decades. A theoretically democratic system declined, under President Sukarno, into an apparently unrestricted presidential system before he was toppled from power in the late 1960s by the Indonesian army, led by his successor, President Suharto. Even before this dramatic development, regional dissatisfaction with rule from Jakarta had led to a rebellion against the central government at the end of the 1950s. Despite secret backing from outside forces, civil and military leaders in regional areas, and particularly in Sumatra and Sulawesi, failed in their aims and the authority of the central government in Jakarta was maintained. The rebellion showed, nevertheless, that regional interests were an important feature of Indonesia's society.

The truth of this judgment was underlined by the re-emergence of a 'Free Aceh' movement in northern Sumatra in the 1990s. Aceh has long had a sense of its special identity, marked by a much deeper commitment to a strict observance of Islam than has been the case in much of Java. It is this fact that has led to Aceh being called 'the veranda of Mecca', a popular name emphasising its Islamic devotion and early links with Muslim missionaries who came to Indonesia and converted the Acehenese. Of all the regions in Indonesia that resisted the Dutch colonial advance, none did so more vigorously than Aceh. As a region that contributes greatly to Indonesia's oil wealth, Aceh's population feels that it has not benefited in the proportion it deserves from the services provided by the national budget. And Aceh is not the only region of Indonesia that has questioned the right of the government in Jakarta to make decisions on its behalf. Irian Jaya, or Papua, the western part of the island of New Guinea, is another, while East Timor has shown that it is possible for even a weak but determined population to demand and gain independence from the Indonesian state.

Suharto's authoritarian rule lasted for two decades before resentment of the regime's abuse of human rights and the fundamental weakness of its economic system, revealed in the 1997 Asian economic crisis, led to his fall in 1999. Since then, Indonesia has had three presidents as the country struggles to find a working democratic system of government and to face up to the major problems of separatism in Aceh and Irian Jaya (Papua) and the fact of bitter religious conflict in the Moluccas.

The Philippines has also faced major challenges to its political unity, many of which are related to its geographical circumstances and the split in its population between majority Christians and an important Islamic minority. Under both Spanish and American colonialism the southern islands of the Philippines were a world apart. While the impact of the Catholic Spanish rulers in the northern islands was such that the Philippines is the only country in Southeast Asia with Christianity as the dominant religion, what happened in the south was very different. Islam was already established in the southern islands when the Spanish arrived, and over the centuries, the presence of this religion has reinforced the feeling of the southerners that they are separate from their northern Catholic countrymen. This sense of a separate identity was always a cause for some problems, but as long as the government in Manila, whether Spanish, American, or most recently Filipino, did not try to impose too strict a rule in the south, it seemed possible to balance the interests of the central government and those of the Islamic southerners.

Since independence, and particularly since the 1970s, the government in Manila has increasingly tried to exercise control over the southern Islamic regions. The result has been a long-running struggle that remains unresolved, with on-and-off periods of armed conflict between government and separatist forces. Simply put, this is a clash between a central government determined to control the whole of the nation's territory and those in an outer region of the state who do not share the interests, the religion—in a word, the identity—of those at the centre.

Just as important have been the difficulties arising from unresolved issues about the political system the Philippines adopted at independence. Modelled in part on the United States system of government, with a president and a congress, the Philippines since the Second World War has struggled to find a balance between the powers to be exercised by these two institutions. By the late 1970s, power had passed decisively to the president, Ferdinand Marcos, but his corrupt and dictatorial style led to a popular revolt and he was ousted from office in 1986. Since then, Philippine politics have remained volatile, with another revolt in early 2001 deposing the incumbent president, Joseph Estrada. Meanwhile, Islamic separatists in the southern Philippines continue to challenge the authority of the central government in Manila.

Despite a high degree of stability, neither Brunei nor Singapore, the two smallest states in Southeast Asia, with the exception of East Timor, have totally escaped challenges to national unity, though their political systems have remained essentially unchanged for decades. In Brunei's case, a failed rebellion in the early 1960s cemented in place the Brunei royal family's determination to maintain a system of benign non-parliamentary rule. For Singapore, the issue of national unity has always been related to ethnic divisions within the state. With a dominant ethnic Chinese population (approximately 77 per cent), there has been and is a need to pay due attention to the interests of the ethnic Malay minority (15 per cent) whose Islamic religion sets them apart from the Chinese majority and who are conscious of the nearby presence of Indonesia and Malaysia, where their ethnic cousins and fellow Muslims are the dominant political force. Yet, while these facts remain as a permanent cause for concern, Singapore's closely controlled system of government, marked by a strong authoritarian character in matters of national and personal behaviour, has succeeded in making the island state the most prosperous in the region.

Continuing change

The fact that arrangements put in place at the time of independence for the countries of Southeast Asia have been adjusted to meet new circumstances should not be surprising. Change, after all, has been a continuing feature of other, long-established democracies in the West. Because change has taken place over a relatively short period of time it appears more striking to an outside observer. And in the light of challenges that still exist for all governments in the region, it would not be surprising to see change taking place again. Yet, having said this, and with all the problems that have been noted, there seems every reason to argue that Southeast Asia at the beginning of the twenty-first century faces the future with greater hope for stability than was the case fifty years ago.

It is easy to use the wrong yardstick in trying to make judgments about Southeast Asia's future. Against the measure of life in the developed countries of the Western world, it would be foolish not to recognise the difficulties Southeast Asian governments and their peoples face. Yet there is another yardstick that should be kept in mind. The problems of the present should be measured against the problems of the past. Consider the problems that faced the countries of Southeast Asia forty years ago. Just to list the most obvious problems of that time. Vietnam was in the early phases of a war that was not to end until 1975; Indonesia was sinking deeper into economic crisis under the erratic leadership of President Sukarno; Malaysia had only recently declared an end to the Communist Emergency that had lasted from 1948 to 1960; and Singapore, nowadays a shining example of economic success—whatever reservations some outsiders may have about the nature of its political system—was still not independent, its economy underdeveloped, and the majority of its population living in decaying slum housing.

Throughout Southeast Asia there were major health problems which, even if they have not yet been eliminated, have now been greatly reduced. (HIV-AIDS is the great qualification to this observation.) Farming methods have improved, not least because of the widespread use of high-yield rice varieties and of agricultural pumps to assist in irrigation. 'Walking tractors', the multi-purpose agricultural machine that can be managed by one person, have made the farming of crops much more efficient. Many more Southeast Asians are being educated at the beginning of the 21st century than was the case forty years ago, even if there is room for improvement in the availability of schools and in the extension of education beyond the primary level. The availability of transport has increased dramatically in four decades, and Southeast Asians have been quick to take advantage of this fact. Nowhere can this be seen more strikingly than in Thailand, where fleets of air-conditioned buses travel the highways in place of the uncomfortable motor transport of earlier years. Southeast Asian cities have changed, almost out of recognition. Many would argue this is a mixed blessing, since change has often meant the loss of older picturesque buildings and new problems linked to traffic congestion and environmental pollution. Nevertheless, the changes that have occurred in Southeast Asia's cities are the result of expanding economies, however much these have been subjected to financial stress, and even serious crises, such as those that affected Southeast Asia—and Asia more generally—at the end of the 1990s.

So there are reasons for optimism, as well as causes for concern and even pessimism. From the point of view of Southeast Asians themselves, the future is open and the prospect of uncertainties ahead is more than balanced by the fact of being free of the colonial rule that existed throughout the region only sixty years ago. To have achieved so much in the years since independence underlines the strength of Southeast Asia's dynamic character.

13

Southeast Asia's living past

Throughout their long history, the peoples of Southeast Asia have shown great strength of purpose and a capacity for enormous physical energy. This has been apparent in the tireless efforts of peasants working in their fields and in the dedication of great leaders. The great temple buildings of the past testify to local genius and organisation. But so, too, do the drained river deltas brought into cultivation and the rice terraces built on steep slopes when no other land was available for cultivation. At another level, the commercial triumphs of the descendants of immigrant Chinese, who have risen from poverty to become tycoons measuring their wealth in billions of dollars, is a reflection of the energy to be found in the region.

The age of great religious monuments such as Angkor, Pagan and Prambanan has passed, never to be repeated, but the same concentrated purpose than went into the construction of these mighty symbols of faith lives on in other ways: in the capacity shown by Cambodians to rebuild their shattered country after the terrible Pol Pot years; in the determination of an increasingly young population throughout the region to demand more democratic forms of government; and in the readiness of Southeast Asians to come to terms with the march of globalisation while maintaining solid links with their own traditions and cultures.

Southeast Asians and their own history

How do Southeast Asians view their own history? Not surprisingly, a correct answer would seem to be that they view it in many different ways. In Vietnam, there is a concern with the details of past events. This is seen in the presence in every major Vietnamese city of a Hai Ba Trung Street (The Two Sisters Trung Street), a street commemorating the heroic deeds of two sisters who led a rebellion against the Chinese in the first century. And the importance of this event will be known to every Vietnamese school child. At the same time, and in a manner similar to the writing of history in other communist states, history in Vietnam is written in a fashion that pays careful attention to national ideology. Elsewhere, by contrast, in countries such as Cambodia, Burma and Indonesia, there is a tendency, at the popular level at least, to view past history in a manner that places as much importance on magical forces as on verifiable facts. Legend and reality are intertwined.

But no matter how the past is perceived, it would be a major error for an outsider to the region to dismiss the importance of history for Southeast Asians because their approach to history can differ from the 'scientific' approach of the West. This was a mistake made by the French colonialists who came to Cambodia in the nineteenth century. They could not believe that the king who ruled over the impoverished Cambodian court of the time could be descended from the rulers who centuries before had built the mighty temples of Angkor. And, just as importantly, they failed to recognise that memories of Angkor, transformed though they may have been into legend, remained important to the Cambodians of a later time. As an example, the last king of Cambodia to reign before the French established their colonial control, Ang Duang, issued coins that displayed the distinctive profile of Angkor Wat's towers. He and his subjects did not have a Western understanding of Angkorian history, but they knew that the temples were an important part of *their* past. In modern times, the profile of Angkor Wat's towers has appeared on all Cambodian flags since independence, including the flag flown by Pol Pot's Khmer Rouge regime.

An ever-growing amount of research into Southeast Asian history is being carried out in a scientific or Western-style fashion in the universities of the region. But for the general population of most of Southeast Asia, their interest in the past is just as real, if different from the approach found in the West. This can be seen in many ways. The Indonesian population of Palembang in southern Sumatra did not know of the existence of Srivijaya, the great trading empire that flourished along the Straits of Malacca between the seventh and fourteenth centuries, until a Western historian rediscovered its existence in the early twentieth century. Today the name 'Srivijaya' is found in multiple uses in Palembang, from schools and shops to a military base. Here is an example of rediscovered history being adopted with a sense of pride in what was previously a forgotten past. Once again, the detail of that past is not what matters. What is important is the fact that the people of Palembang, and more generally, of Indonesia, are ready to embrace history for the sense it gives of a continuity between the past and the present.

Laos provides another example of this desire to link past and present. For the people of Laos, the exact nature of the state of Lan Xang, which incorporated much of the territory of modern Laos between the fourteenth and seventeenth centuries, is less important than the vision they have of the importance of this kingdom as a forerunner of the Lao state today. And this is an interest in the past of their country that is shared by Lao of whatever political persuasion.

Living traditions

In contemporary Southeast Asia, traditional means more than simply having a memory of the past. Instead, tradition is part of a living present which is found in ceremonies and festivals, in drama and in puppet theatre. Hindu epics such as the *Ramayana* and *Mahabharata* have been transformed into popular entertainments. These great legendary stories form the core of the *wayang kulit* shadow puppet theatre of Indonesia. This is an outstanding example of a cultural tradition that has not only survived into modern times, but which continues to be seen as having magical qualities while also providing a commentary on political issues of the day. For while the puppet actors appear in stylised traditional form, and act out their familiar parts, their *dalang*, the puppeteer, mixes comments on the politics of the day with the unfolding stories of the epics.

In Thailand and Cambodia, the tale of the *Ramayana*, presented as a dance drama, continues to fascinate audiences for its reflection of the never-ending clash between the forces of good and evil in the world. This is true whether the performance takes place in the glittering surrounds of a royal court or in a shabby provincial setting. In a manner that is sometimes hard for an outsider to grasp, there is a spiritual character to these popular entertainments that is lacking in the secular West. Perhaps to understand this, a Westerner has to think of how the morality plays of medieval Europe were viewed at a time when the power and role of the Christian religion were very different from what they are today.

Visitors to Southeast Asia are captivated by the traditional dances performed throughout the region, ranging from hearty

Traditional court dances still take place in Cambodia, where the royal ballet has now been reconstituted following the dreadful years of the Pol Pot tyranny.

country routines danced by enthusiastic peasant farmers to the refined perfection of court performances at such varied locations as Phnom Penh in Cambodia and Surakarta (Solo) in central Java. The revival of the traditional ballet of the Cambodian court after the devastation of the Pol Pot years is another example of Southeast Asian resilience. Once again, Cambodian dancers dressed in the richest silks shot through with gold and silver thread and wearing golden tiered crowns or the masks of fantastic beasts perform a repertoire derived from the Hindu epics. In movements that conjure up the carvings to be seen at Angkor, gestures with hand and finger can mean as much as sudden movements of the whole body. In some cases, such as when the monkey gods join in battle in an episode from the *Ramayana*, the dances are realistic to an almost buffoonish degree. At other times, the movements of the individuals and groups are as abstract yet as disciplined as those of a wheeling flock of birds.

A traditional Cambodian silk pidan, *or cloth hanging, depicting heavenly nymphs and elephants linked to stories of the Buddha's life.*

The richly varied textiles of Southeast Asia provide a striking example of the continuing blending of the past and present in the region. No matter how common it might be to see Western-style clothing in Southeast Asia's cities, traditional textiles remain an important part of life. Nowhere is this more apparent than in Java, where *batik* cloth remains both a vital part of dress and an art form that is full of cultural meaning. In some cases the motifs that are used draw on traditions that date back to prehistoric times. This is the case with the 'broken sword' pattern that is particularly associated with royal and noble families in central Java. It is a motif that symbolically protects the wearer from evil. The long-time presence of Chinese traders in the northern coastal region of Cirebon in Java is reflected in the batiks of that city with their abstract representations of rocks and clouds. These are objects full of mystical symbolism in Chinese culture, but here they are adapted as an Indonesian motif.

In some cases the symbolism of the motifs that decorate Southeast Asian textiles are difficult for an outsider to recognise. At other times, as with the decorative hanging cloths of Cambodia, the *pidan*, the basic pictorial elements illustrating scenes from the life of the Buddha and depicting heavenly nymphs or elephants, are readily recognisable.

History, culture and tradition live on in Southeast Asia. They are at the heart of a fascinating world that waits to be explored. And, at the beginning of the 21st century, there is now so much more of Southeast Asia that *can* be explored than was possible until very recently. The temples of Angkor were 'forbidden territory' for nearly two decades as a result of conflict in Cambodia. Laos kept its borders closed to foreign visitors until the end of the 1980s, preventing access to such major cultural sites as the former royal city of Luang Prabang and the Angkorian-period temples at Wat Phu in the far south of the country. Travel in Burma, too, has become progressively easier over the past decade, as has travel in Vietnam.

Above all, Southeast Asia rewards a visitor who responds to the region on its own terms, conscious of the past and open to its present. Great temple complexes and abandoned cities are only one aspect of the past, just as the crowded cities of contemporary Southeast Asia provide only one insight into the region's modern identity. The deeper a visitor penetrates in this complex world, the greater the opportunity to grasp the many strands that have shaped Southeast Asia's vibrant culture and contributed to its modern character. With a knowledge of Southeast Asia's past history, the present becomes both more understandable and so more readily appreciated. This is a world that richly rewards a sympathetic visitor.

History at a glance

Below are country-by-country summaries of Southeast Asia's history. Major events are highlighted and statistics are provided for the current population of each country.

Brunei

Modern Brunei traces its history back to earlier states on the north coast of the island of Borneo. Chinese traders visited Brunei as early as the **6th century** CE. When the Chinese admiral, Cheng Ho, visited Brunei in the early **15th century** he reported it was an active trading centre. By that time the Sultan of Brunei had converted to Islam.

Under Sultan Bolkiah **(1473–1521)** Brunei was one of the most powerful regional states in maritime Southeast Asia. Its importance as a trading state grew after Portugal conquered Malacca in **1511**. But by the beginning of the **18th century**, power was slipping away from Brunei's rulers. Dutch commercial power slowly undermined Brunei's trading role and the foundation of Singapore in **1819** meant Brunei could not recapture its former glory. The population of Brunei declined and numbered only 10 000 in the **1830s**.

In the **19th century** Brunei lost control over Sarawak to James Brooke, the first of the 'white rajahs', and Sabah to the British North Borneo Company. Its survival as a state was finally assured when Britain declared it a protectorate in **1888**.

Brunei's fortunes were transformed by the discovery of oil and natural gas in its territory in the **1920s**. After the Second World War, revenue from oil and gas made Brunei the richest state, per capita, in Southeast Asia.

It declined to join Malaysia in **1963**, fearing that to do so would lead to a loss of its revenues to the new federation.

Britain remained as the protecting power until **1984**, when Brunei became independent. It joined ASEAN the same year.

Brunei has a population of approximately 290 000 persons, made up of Malays 67 per cent, Chinese 20 per cent and tribal peoples 8 per cent. The balance of the population is composed of guest workers, mostly from the Philippines.

Burma

The recorded history of Burma (officially the Union of Myanmar) begins in the **5th century** CE, when states emerged in the delta of the Irrawaddy River. These were populated by non-Burmans and were deeply influenced by India. Burmans, migrating from the north, arrived in the **11th century** and founded a state at Pagan **c.1140**. It was the centre of a powerful empire until it was sacked by the Mongols, who were ruling China, in **1287**.

During the next three centuries a series of minor states competed for influence over the territories once ruled from Pagan. In the middle of the **16th century**, an energetic new ruler, Bayinnaung, took power in Pegu, near Rangoon, and gained control over much of lower Burma. In a reign of thirty-one years **(1550–81)**, Bayinnaung extended Burmese power into modern Laos and Thailand and actively promoted Buddhism. But following his death, the Pegu kingdom rapidly declined. Once again, Burma fragmented into a series of small competing states.

From the middle of the **18th century**, there was a revival of central power under the Konbaung Dynasty based at Ava, near Mandalay, led by King Alungpaya **(1752–60)**. His successors expanded Ava's power and for a period dominated northern Laos and defeated their Thai rivals, capturing Ayuthia in **1767**. For a period, Burma was the strongest state in mainland Southeast Asia, but by the beginning of the **19th century**, its power was declining and it had become inward-looking.

From the beginning of the **19th century**, the Burmese rulers faced a new challenge with the expansion of British interests into territories in north-east India which the court at Ava regarded as within its sphere of influence. This clash of interests resulted in the First Burma War **(1824–26)** and the establishment of a British colonial presence along Burmese territory fronting the Bay of Bengal. Further confrontations between the Burmese and the British led to the Second Burma War **(1852–53)** and the Third Burma War

(1885) and to the control of the whole of modern Burma as a British colony. The colonising British abolished the Burmese monarchy

Until 1937 Burma was ruled as part of British India. With colonial encouragement, Burma became an important exporter of rice and timber. Because of its administrative link with India, there was large-scale immigration of Indians into Burma. Resentment of this immigration was one of the factors stimulating the emergence of a Burmese nationalist movement in the 1930s.

When Japan invaded Burma in 1942, it was initially welcomed by many in the population, including a group of young army officers led by Aung San. Welcome soon turned to resentment when it became clear that Japan was behaving like another colonial power and was ready to resort to brutal measures to advance its interests. By the end of the war, Aung San and his associates were working to defeat the Japanese.

Britain returned to Burma promising independence and this was achieved in 1948, but not before Aung San and six of his closest associates were assassinated in July 1947. Independent Burma was wracked by political factionalism and the long-term problems of difficult relations between the majority Burmese and the country's ethnic minorities. In 1962, the military, led by General New Win, overthrew U Nu's civilian government and under various names the military has remained in power ever since.

Large-scale protests against military rule occurred in 1988 and were suppressed with great violence. An election held in 1990 resulted in a victory by the National League for Democracy, led by Aung San Suu Kyi. But these were declared null and void and Aung San Suu Kyi was placed under house arrest for two lengthy periods, before finally being released in 2002. Although now technically free, her movements are controlled and the military show no signs of yielding its position to its civilian political opponents.

Burma became a member of ASEAN in 1997.

The population of Burma is 48 million, of which ethnic Burmese account for approximately 67 per cent.

Cambodia

Modern Cambodia traces its origins back to the state of Funan that emerged in the 3rd century CE. It was a state that absorbed considerable cultural influence from India. In the 6th century, Funan faded from view to be succeeded by Chenla whose rulers can be identified as Khmer (Cambodian) predecessors of the later rulers of Angkor.

Founded by Jayavarman II (802–c.834), the Angkorian empire flourished from the 9th to the 14th century. Its rulers built the magnificent temples at its political centre that still remain so impressive today and extended their power over much of the territory of modern Thailand, Vietnam and Laos. Its most outstanding rulers in the centuries after Jayavarman II were Suryavarman II **(1113–50)**, who built Angkor Wat, and Jayavarman VII **(1118–c.1218)**, who constructed more temples than any other Angkorian ruler, including the Bayon at the centre of his royal city, Angkor Thom.

The Angkorian empire was not a commercial power, for its existence it depended on the loyalty of those who governed its far-flung possessions. When the Thais began to challenge the authority of the ruler at Angkor in the **13th century**, it entered a period of slow decline. The eventual abandonment of Angkor took place around the middle of the **15th century**. From that date on, the Cambodian capital was located either in or close to the site of modern Phnom Penh.

Cambodia was still an important regional power in the **mid-17th century**, but from that time onwards it was squeezed between the expanding states of Vietnam and Thailand. By the early **19th century**, Cambodia had almost ceased to exist as Thai and Vietnamese power grew ever stronger. It was a small impoverished kingdom when the French established a protectorate over it in **1863**.

The French gradually assumed more and more control over Cambodian affairs, but they left the king in place and maintained his symbolic importance for the Cambodian population. This was to be of great significance for modern Cambodian history.

By the beginning of the Second World War, the French in Cambodia had presided over modest economic development of rubber plantations and the expansion of rice-growing for export production. Little effort was made to expand education and by the end of the **1930s**, fewer than twelve Cambodians had completed a full high school education. Until the **1940s**, there was no significant nationalist movement in Cambodia.

The French placed Norodom Sihanouk on the Cambodian throne in **1941** with the expectation that he would be a cooperative figure in the difficult years of the Second World War, when the Japanese allowed the French to maintain their administration throughout Indochina. Following the end of the war and with the re-establishment of French control, Sihanouk matured politically and by the beginning of the **1950s** he had become the leader of Cambodia's push for independence. France granted Cambodia independence in **1953**.

Abdicating the throne to become a full-time politician in **1955**, Sihanouk was the dominant figure in Cambodia until the late **1960s**. By that time the country was in economic decline and Sihanouk's dealings with the North Vietnamese communists had alienated Sihanouk's right-wing supporters. They toppled him in a coup d'état in **1970**, an event that was followed by the outbreak of a full-scale civil war which lasted until **1975** with the victory of the radical Cambodian communist regime led by Pol Pot.

The terrible tyranny of the Pol Pot regime lasted until **1979** and resulted in the death of upwards of two million persons, perhaps 500 000 of these through executions. After a further decade of war, peace finally returned to Cambodia at the end of the **1980s**, with the involvement of the United Nations. Since **1993**, Hun Sen has been Cambodia's prime minister, while Sihanouk was once again crowned king in the same year. Cambodia joined ASEAN in **1997**.

The population of Cambodia is 11 million.

East Timor

The existence of Timor as a source of sandalwood is known from early Chinese records dating from periods well before the first European contact with the island in the **16th century**. The first Portuguese reference to Timor dates from **1514**, but it may not have been until **1516** that a Portuguese ship actually visited the island. The first permanent Portuguese settlement in the region, on a nearby island and not on Timor itself, dates from the **1560s**.

It was not until the middle of the **17th century** that Portuguese in any numbers—at most, a few hundred—had settled in Timor, with many of these settlers members of religious orders. By this stage the Dutch were active in the Indonesian archipelago and in **1653** they succeeded in pushing the Portuguese out of their small settlement at Kupang in the west of the island. After operating from a base at Lifau in the Oecusse region of the island for a period, the Portuguese moved their administrative capital to Dili in **1769.**

Distant from Portugal and with limited resources, the settlement in East Timor became a neglected part of Portugal's overseas empire. Located near the much stronger Dutch possessions, it seemed frequently at risk of being absorbed by the Dutch. But its existence was preserved by treaties concluded with the Dutch in **1859** and **1893**.

In the **20th century**, the Portuguese government did little to develop its colony in Timor. Producing little of value for export, it was used as a location to which political opponents of the state could be deported. Although Portugal was neutral during the Second World War, the Japanese invaded East Timor in **1942** in response to Australian military activity there.

Following the war, Portugal continued to rule East Timor until revolution in Portugal led to the colonial administrations deserting the island in **1974**. This event set the stage for civil war in the abandoned colony and to

Indonesia's invading East Timor in **1975**. Jakarta justified its invasion on the basis that it feared an independent East Timor would be pro-communist.

East Timor was incorporated into the Indonesian state in **1976**, but despite a large Indonesian military presence and often brutal suppression of opposition to its occupation, Indonesia was never able to overcome the guerrilla movement that fought for the goal of Timorese independence.

International criticism of Indonesian behaviour in East Timor, which increased after the fall of President Suharto in **1998,** led to his successor, B. J. Habibie, offering the Timorese the opportunity to vote for or against independence in a ballot held in **1999**. Despite Indonesian intimidation, the East Timorese voted overwhelmingly in favour of independence. The vote was followed by the introduction into East Timor of a temporary United Nations administration to prepare the territory for independence. East Timor became independent in **2002**.

The population of East Timor is estimated to be 800 000.

Indonesia

Indonesia's territorial boundaries are a creation of the colonial period, since before the establishment of Dutch rule there was no single pre-colonial state that controlled the whole of the Indonesian archipelago.

The earliest kingdoms to exist in what is now Indonesia were located in Java and Sumatra. By the **7th century**, powerful land kingdoms had emerged in central Java that built the major Buddhist and Hindu temples located near Yogyakarta that can still be seen today. A very different, maritime kingdom known as Srivijaya controlled the passage of trade through the Straits of Malacca. By the **14th century**, the power of these early kingdoms had faded and, with the exception of Bali, where the Hindu religion lived on, Islam was slowly but steadily becoming the dominant religion. Islam had first arrived in Indonesia in the **13th century**.

The first Europeans to make contact with the Indonesian region were the Portuguese who arrived in the **16th century**, drawn by the prospect of gaining control of the spice trade. In the **17th century**, the Dutch replaced the Portuguese as the major foreign power in the region, but their control of territory was very limited and the existing Indonesian sultanates continued to rule with little interference from the European newcomers. It was not until the **18th century** that the Dutch began to become a territorial power, steadily increasing their control over most of Java. Yet by the end of the **18th century**, most of modern Indonesia still lay outside Dutch control. The second half of the **19th century** was when the major Dutch advance throughout the archipelago took place, with some territories, including Bali, only coming under Dutch control at the beginning of the **20th century**.

Dutch colonialism had an enormous impact on the Indonesian population as the administration based in Batavia (modern Jakarta) tried to exact the maximum economic benefit from the territories it controlled. During the **19th century**, the colonial administration required villages to provide a set amount of certain agricultural commodities for export—in particular, sugar, tea and coffee. Later, in the early years of the **20th century**, Sumatra was transformed through the establishment of rubber and tobacco plantations. Both in Java and in Sumatra the colonial economic system gave only minimal reward to the local population. With a growing population and a limited availability of land, poverty became entrenched in some areas of Java.

The inequities in the colonial system brought a nationalist reaction by the **1920s**, as young, educated Indonesians questioned the Dutch right to rule and the nature of the economic arrangements which saw rewards going almost exclusively to the Dutch and immigrant Chinese. Prominent among the early nationalists were Sukarno and Mohammad Hatta. Both were jailed by the Dutch in the **1930s** as the colonial power kept a tight control over any activity suggesting Indonesia should become independent.

The Japanese invasion and occupation of Indonesia during the Second World War **(1942–45)** laid the ground for the Indonesian push for independence once the war ended. Not only had the Dutch been humiliated, but nationalists, such as Sukarno, were able to pursue their goals of working for an independent Indonesia. When the Dutch returned at the end of the war, they faced a determined nationalist movement that was ready to fight for the independence which Sukarno had declared in **August 1945**.

Fighting between the Indonesians and the Dutch continued until **1949**, when the Dutch finally withdrew leaving Indonesia with a severely damaged economy. Initially, the country held together under Sukarno's charismatic leadership, supported by the power of the Indonesian army. But the political system was under severe strain as the result of a lack of shared policy aims among competing groups, particularly the Indonesian Communist Party and the army. With the economy in tatters, an attempted coup in **1965** brought a harsh army reaction and the killing of some hundreds of thousands of communists and their alleged allies. Sukarno was stripped of power and was succeeded as president by General Suharto in **1967** at the head of what was called the New Order government.

At one level, Suharto's rule was highly successful as economic decline was reversed and the level of poverty among the population dramatically decreased. But these achievements came at the cost of authoritarian rule and the toleration of widespread corruption, including in the president's own family and among civil and military officials close to the centre of power.

Suharto's firm anticommunist stance was welcomed by West, and in particular by the United States, a fact that enabled Indonesia's invasion of East Timor in **1975** to take place with a minimum of international criticism.

By the **mid-1990s**, it had become clear that major problems lay beneath the prosperity that Suharto's government had engineered. Increasing authoritarianism was resented by a growing middle class, and in particular by the large number of students who found that their education was not a guarantee of a future job. As revelations of ever-increasing corruption circulated, some of Suharto's key associates distanced themselves from the president. Then, in the face of widespread demonstrations against his rule and the withdrawal of the crucial support of the army, Suharto was forced to resign in **May 1998**. Subsequently, new laws were introduced to make Indonesia's political system more democratic.

Since Suharto's fall there have been three presidents of Indonesia in rapid succession—first Suharto's former vice-president, B. J. Habibie, then Wahid Abdurrahman, and finally Megawati Sukarnoputri, the daughter of Indonesia's first president.

Indonesia was a founding member of ASEAN in **1967**.

Indonesia has a population of 220 million.

Laos

In its modern territorial form, Laos is a creation of the colonial period when France imposed its control at the end of the **19th century**, but in historical terms, Laos can be regarded as a successor to the Lan Xang kingdom ('Kingdom of One Million Elephants') founded by King Fa Ngum in **1353**. Lan Xang was originally a tributary state linked to Angkor, but it grew in power with Angkor's decline. Despite frequently difficult relations with stronger neighbours—Burma, Thailand and Vietnam—it survived and reached the height of its success during the reign of Souligna Vongsa **(1637–94)**. During this time, Vientiane was regarded as one of the richest in mainland Southeast Asia.

Following Souligna Vongsa's death, Lan Xang fragmented into a series of small states. The three most important were located along the Mekong River: Luang Prabang, Vientiane and Champassak. Not only were these rival to each other, their rulers had to contend with interference in their affairs by the same more powerful neighbours who had troubled the Lan Xang kingdom. By the early **19th century**, Vientiane was the most powerful of the Lao principalities. Its king, Chao Anou, initially had good relations with the Thai court, but in **1826** he invaded Thai territory. Bangkok reacted swiftly and harshly, sacking Vientiane in **1827** and again the following year, and either killing or driving the city's population into slavery. For the rest of the **19th century**, the Lao territories became a backwater region with the Mekong River principalities acknowledging their subordinate status by paying tribute to their stronger regional neighbours.

Change came with the determination of the French to prevent the British gaining control of territory in the Lao regions to the north and west of their colonial possessions in Cambodia and Vietnam. From **1893** onwards, with a remarkable French official, Auguste Pavie, playing a central role, France established a colonial presence in Laos. By **1904**, France controlled the territories of modern Laos, with Vientiane as its administrative capital. The ruler of Luang Prabang was proclaimed the King of Laos, with Luang Prabang the royal capital. The royal families of Vientiane and Champassak were also accorded a special status within this new set of colonial political arrangements.

As the colonial power in Laos, France did little to develop the country economically. The status of the traditional elite was preserved, but Vietnamese were employed in the lower levels of the country's administration. At no time during the French colonial period did the number of Frenchmen resident in Laos exceed 1000. There was no significant nationalist agitation in Laos in the **1920s** and **1930s**.

The Second World War acted as a spur to nationalism, so that when the war ended and France tried to re-establish its position in Laos, it found that there was now a group of anti-colonial Lao, some of whom had embraced communism. Prominent among the communists was Prince Souphanouvong who had developed close links with the Vietnamese Communist Party. When Laos gained independence from France in **1953**, the Lao communists were sufficiently powerful that provision was made for them to be made part of the independent country's armed forces and its administration.

This provision failed, as did attempts to incorporate the Lao communists into a neutralist coalition government. From **1954** until **1975**, royalist, neutralist and communist factions jockeyed for position as Laos became increasingly involved in the Vietnam War. Repeated efforts to find a neutralist solution for Laos failed, but in **1973**, agreement was reached to establish a national coalition government. Playing their cards skilfully, the communists steadily increased their power so that, following the communist victories in Cambodia and Vietnam, they too were able to take power in November **1975**.

The communists dealt harshly with those they saw as class enemies, sending upwards of 40 000 to re-education camps. They attempted to minimise the power of the Buddhist church and effectively closed Laos off to the outside world. Since the late **1980s**, the Lao government has relaxed many of its harsher measures in the economic field but has shown no interest in relaxing its tight political control over the population. Conscious of its need for foreign exchange, the government has opened the country to tourism. Laos became a member of ASEAN in **1997**.

Laos has a population of 5 million.

Malaysia

Modern Malaysia is a federation of a number of territories that were part of Britain's colonial empire in the **19th** and **20th centuries**. These were the sultanates of peninsular Malaya; Penang and Malacca, which with Singapore once formed part of the Straits Settlements; and the Borneo territories of Sabah and Sarawak.

Knowledge of the early history of all of these regions is limited, but by the **15th century**, we know of the existence of Malacca, on the west coast of modern peninsular Malaysia. A major trading centre, Malacca was, in some fashion, a successor of the earlier maritime trading state of Srivijaya, whose capital was in southern Sumatra. Malacca was a vital link in trade between the maritime world and the Indian sub-continent and was at the height of its powers when the Portuguese captured it in **1511**.

In the period following Portugal's conquest of Malacca, the sultanates of the Malayan peninsula competed with each other for local dominance and, on occasion, made temporary alliances with external powers. In Borneo, the Brunei sultanate controlled the areas that became Sabah and Sarawak and was at its strongest in the late **16th** and early **17th centuries**.

The **18th century** was a period of instability in the Malayan world and in **1786**, the first British colonial intrusion took advantage of this fact with the founding of a colony in Penang. This development was followed by the foundation of Singapore in **1819** and the establishment of Sarawak as a 'private' British colonial enterprise in the **1840s**.

Beginning in the **1870s**, Britain slowly advanced into the Malayan Peninsula, establishing colonial control over its sultanates, a process that was completed in the early **20th century**. In Borneo, Brunei was made a British protectorate in **1888**, and in the same year Britain also assumed a protecting role in relation to Sarawak and North Borneo (modern Sabah), where government was in the hands of a chartered company (a British commercial operation operating with the approval of the British government).

These arrangements continued until the Second World War with separate administrative arrangements for the various territories. Of the Straits Settlements (Penang, Malacca and Singapore), Singapore was the commercial powerhouse, the centre for British commercial interests and a major entrepôt. On the Peninsula, tin-mining and rubber production became major export commodities and, until the depression of the **1930s**, made Malaya one of the most productive colonies anywhere in the world.

All the British territories, but with peninsular Malaya and Singapore at the forefront, attracted immigrants from China, and to a lesser extent from India. Their presence was to become a major political problem after the Second World War as the indigenous Malay inhabitants sought to ensure their political dominance.

The Japanese occupation of all of Britain's colonial territories during the Second World War was a watershed event, leading to a realisation, once the Japanese had been defeated, that colonial rule could not continue indefinitely. Malaya gained independence in **1957** with a constitution that gave political power to the Malays while commercial power was left largely in the hands of the immigrant Chinese. As Britain prepared to withdraw entirely from the region, Singapore and the Borneo territories of Sarawak and Sabah joined with Malaya to form the Federation of Malaysia in **1963**. Because of major differences between Singapore and the Malay politicians who ruled in Kuala Lumpur, Singapore was expelled from Malaysia in **1965**.

Serious race riots in **1969** led to a review of Malaysia's constitutional arrangements and the introduction of affirmative action programs, known as the New Economic Policy, designed to improve Malay participation in the commercial world and to increase Malay participation in higher education.

Under long-serving Prime Minister Dr Mahathir Mohamed, power has been centralised in the federal government. Malaysia was a founding member of ASEAN in **1967**.

Malaysia has a population of 22 million.

The Philippines

Very little is known about the Philippines before the first European contact in the **16th century**, for the indigenous inhabitants of the islands that make up the country did not keep written records. From a limited number of Chinese accounts that pre-date European contact, it is clear that Chinese junks traded with the northern Philippines, exchanging local products for silks and porcelains. Islam had reached the southern Philippines by the late **15th century** and by middle of the **16th century** Islam had won converts in the southern islands and reached as far north as the region around modern Manila. As best can be reconstructed from accounts written after European contact, the Philippines in the pre-colonial period was inhabited by a population that lived in social units that were mostly no larger than a village. Certainly, no major state such as had existed in Cambodia or Java in the early historical period was ever established in the Philippines before the arrival of the Spanish.

The first European contact with the Philippines was made by the Spanish explorer Magellan, who reached the island of Cebu in **1521**, but it was not until **1565** that the Spanish returned to Cebu to establish a permanent base in the islands. In **1571**, the Spanish moved their headquarters to Manila, and this city has remained the Philippines capital to the present day.

Spanish colonialism in the Philippines was quite different to the colonial endeavours in other Southeast Asian states. Most distinctively, the Spanish administration worked hand in hand with the Catholic church and, in doing so, brought into being a system of government that was very similar to what occurred in Latin America. On the one hand, the widespread presence of priests and friars led to the Philippines becoming the only nation in modern Southeast Asia in which the overwhelming majority of the population is Christian (over 90 per cent). On the other hand, the system of land-holding that was encouraged was similar to that in Latin America, with large holdings in the hands of a limited and privileged few who depended on the labour of tenant farmers and day labourers. The powerful families, often of mixed race, which developed under this system in the **18th** and **19th** centuries have remained politically and economically powerful to the present day.

Nationalism developed in the Philippines during the second half of the **19th century**, when Filipinos who had been educated in Spanish demanded the same rights as the Spanish colonialists and a range of political reforms, including the separation of church and state. Following an attempted rebellion in **1896**, the admired leader of the nationalists, Jose Rizal, was executed. The nationalists' hopes for independence were set back when, as a consequence of the Spanish–American War, the United States invaded the Philippines in **1898**. This invasion led to the imposition of American colonial control over the country.

America ruled its new colony with a light hand and from the beginning its presence was widely accepted, particularly by the major land-owning families who saw their interests preserved under the new governing power. Moreover, the United States was sincere in its determination to bring economic and social benefits to the Philippines, particularly by providing extensive funds for education. Almost from the beginning of its rule, the United States was committed to the goal of full independence, and in **1934** it oversaw the establishment of the Philippines Commonwealth, with a promise to grant independence twelve years later.

The Philippines was occupied by the Japanese during the Second World War, and while there was some active guerrilla opposition to the Japanese, many among the elite cooperated with the invaders. Following the end of the war in **1945**, the Philippines gained full independence in **1946** and a democratic system based to a large extent on the American form of government was introduced. Essentially, however, politics was a matter of intra-elite competition with little effort made to deal with the social and economic problems that affected the mass of the population.

Following his election as president in **1965** and **1969**, Ferdinand Marcos declared martial law in **1972** and instituted a period of corrupt, authoritarian rule that lasted until his overthrow in a popular rebellion in **1986**. Neither Marcos nor his successors have been able to eliminate the gross inequities that remain in Philippines society, nor have they found a fully satisfactory way to meet the demands of the Muslim population in the south of the country.

The Philippines was a founding member of ASEAN in **1967**.

The population of the Philippines is 74 million.

Singapore

Taking its modern name from an earlier settlement known as *Singapura* ('Lion City'), Singapore's history before the **19th century** has to be constructed from fragmentary Malay, Chinese and Portuguese records. It seems likely that the island of Singapore was the location of one of the outposts of the early maritime empire of Srivijaya before the **14th century**, and that its key position at the base of the Malayan Peninsula led to its playing a part in the trade that passed through the Malacca Straits to the islands of the Indonesian archipelago. Later it was linked to the great trading city of Malacca, but after the Portuguese capture of Malacca in **1511**, Singapore's importance declined. By the early **17th century**, it had become a sparsely inhabited island, home to a few fishermen and pirates.

When Thomas Stamford Raffles singled out Singapore for settlement in **1819**, it had a maximum of 1000 inhabitants. A driven man, Raffles was determined to found a British settlement in Southeast Asia that would support British trade in the Eastern seas and, in so doing, undermine the commercial success of the Dutch. In terms of the establishment of a trading entrepôt, Raffles's foundation of Singapore proved to be a brilliant success. Within a short time the new settlement was proving a magnet for Chinese immigrants and a favoured base for European commercial firms. Shipping from Europe and India bound for China found that Singapore's location met their needs for provisions and offered unlimited opportunities for trade.

By the **1840s**, any reservations that had originally been held about Singapore's commercial viability had disappeared. Forming part of the Straits Settlements, with Penang and Malacca, its British administration, and in particular its legal system, made it an attractive base from which to transact business throughout Southeast Asia. At the same time, its rapidly growing Chinese population provided, with smaller numbers of Indians and Malays, the labour base for the steady development of the island's infrastructure.

From the middle of the **19th century**, Singapore increasingly became a base for firms doing business with the Malay sultanates on the Peninsula. It was from Singapore that commercial firms financed trade and mining in the Malayan Peninsula, and it was the merchants of Singapore who urged the British government to become involved in the affairs of the Malay sultanates.

In the years from the beginning of the **20th century** to the Second World War, Singapore was a prosperous colony whose lifeblood was trade and commerce. Even in the **1930s**, most of its population were immigrants. Below the veneer of the European, mostly British, administrators and business people, the majority of the population was Chinese, with smaller numbers of Indians and Malays. (The ethnic breakdown was, and is, approximately 77 per cent Chinese, Malays 15 per cent and Indians 6 per cent.) And before the war there was no suggestion that Singapore would become independent.

As elsewhere in Southeast Asia, the Japanese invasion of Singapore in **1942** was a shattering blow to colonial prestige, but when peace was restored in **1945**, the British government was reluctant to include Singapore in its slowly developing plans to grant independence for Malaya. Concerned to maintain Singapore for strategic reasons and disturbed by communist activity in Singapore's trade unions, it did not grant self-government until **1955**. By that stage, the brilliant Chinese lawyer Lee Kuan Yew had emerged as a key political figure. At the head of the People's Action Party (PAP), Lee was prime minister when, in **1963**, Singapore gained independence and joined the new Federation of Malaysia.

In **1965**, Singapore was expelled from Malaysia. From the point of view of the Malay politicians who dominated politics in Kuala Lumpur, Singapore as an ethnically Chinese state could not be accommodated in the federation. Since separation, Singapore politics have been dominated by the PAP, which has been remarkably successful in building a modern city state in which economic success is balanced against a readiness to use authoritarian methods to implement and maintain government policies.

Singapore was a founding member of ASEAN in **1967**.
Singapore's population is 3.9 million.

Thailand

The only country in Southeast Asia never to have been colonised, modern
Thailand (known as Siam for most of its existence) traces its history back
to the emergence of small kingdoms in the central plains region of the
modern kingdom in the **13th century**. Previously, this region of modern Thailand was occupied by the Mon people, but from as early as the **7th century**,
Tai-speaking immigrants had moved steadily south into Thailand from the
southwestern Chinese province of Yunnan.

The most important of the early Thai states was Sukhothai, which initially
was a vassal of the great Angkorian empire. Today, Sukhothai, with its most
important ruler Ramkhamhaeng **(c.1279–98)**, is regarded as the birthplace
of the modern Thai state. As Sukhothai's power declined, another Thai state
emerged at Ayuthia in the **mid-14th century**. By this stage the Thais were
challenging Angkor's political dominion, but their cultural debt to Angkor was
considerable.

Ayuthia was at the centre of an increasingly powerful Thai kingdom from
1351 to **1767**, when the Burmese sacked the city and the Thai court moved
further south to a location near modern Bangkok. Before this time, the rulers
at Ayuthia expanded their control over much of the territory of modern Thailand and Laos and carried on an active commercial relationship with traders
from various European countries.

After the sack and abandonment of Ayuthia, a military leader, Taksin,
assumed the throne and began rebuilding the state. Resentment of his tyrannical behaviour led to his being overthrown in **1782** when he was replaced
by Rama I, the first of the Chakri Dynasty that still rules in Thailand today.
Under Rama I, Bangkok was founded in **1782** and the new king showed a
remarkable talent for recruiting able men to oversee the good administration of his kingdom. This talent was inherited by his successors in the
19th century, and, in particular, by Rama IV, King Mongkut **(1851–68)**, and
Rama V, King Chulalongkorn **(1868–1910)**.

Of the greatest importance for Thailand's survival as an independent
state was the capacity to deal with European nations that Mongkut, Chulalongkorn and their advisers demonstrated. With an awareness of the power
of these nations, the Thai kings were prepared to make concessions when
necessary to maintain their country's independence at the same time as the
court in Bangkok strengthened its control over the kingdom. Of great

importance, too, was the way in which these rulers oversaw the spread of education and development of rural industries, particularly rice and timber for export.

Until **1932**, Thailand existed as an absolute monarchy, but in that year young officers in the army mounted a bloodless coup that drastically reduced the power of the king. Although they introduced a parliamentary system, the Thai military was, in fact, the supreme power in the kingdom. From **1932** until the late **1960s**, the military remained the dominant political force in Thailand.

During the Second World War, the Thai government cooperated with the Japanese, but as the tide of battle turned against the Japanese, and with a Free Thai movement opposing this cooperation, Thai leaders began to prepare for an allied victory.

Reconciled with the victorious Allies, post-war Thailand became an important member of the anti-communist coalition in Southeast Asia. Despite various attempts to introduce a more democratic system, military domination of politics continued until **1973**. In that year, a student-led revolt brought a short period of democratic rule until the army resumed power in **1976**. Elections in **1979** brought the reintroduction of a form of parliamentary rule, which survived attempted coups in **1981** and **1985**. When after further elections in **1992** it appeared that there would be a return to military-dominated rule, there were widespread student protests. These were suppressed with much loss of life, but the military's actions at this time discredited it and when fresh elections were held later in the same year, a civilian-led government took power. The military remains an important, but no longer dominant, element in Thai politics.

Since **1992** Thai politics have remained volatile, but the parliamentary system has continued. Moreover, the country has made considerable economic progress, though this was severely dented by the Asian economic crisis of 1996–97. Throughout its recent history, the role of the Thai King, the ninth ruler of the Chakri Dynasty, King Bhumibol, has been of great importance. At times of crisis, he has played a vital moderating role, and he remains almost universally regarded as the embodiment of the Thai state.

Thailand was a founding member of ASEAN in **1967**.

Thailand's population is 63 million.

Vietnam

The modern Vietnamese state traces its origins to the **2nd century** BCE, when a state with an identifiably ethnic Vietnamese population was absorbed into the Han Chinese empire. Vietnam remained under Chinese control until **931** CE. This long period under Chinese rule led to the absorbing by Vietnam of major aspects of Chinese culture, so that in many ways China was a 'model' for the independent Vietnamese state. It was the only country in Southeast Asia to be deeply influenced by Chinese, as opposed to Indian, culture.

Apart from a short period in the **15th century (1407–28)** when China again succeeded in imposing its control over Vietnam, the country remained independent until the arrival of the French colonialists in the **19th century**. Its relations with China were always difficult as Vietnam's rulers fended off repeated Chinese efforts to exercise control over its smaller neighbour. A distinctive feature of Vietnam's history from independence to the onset of colonialism was its steady advance from its original base in the Red River Delta into lands in the south. In the process of this southward movement, it overwhelmed the previously important state of Champa on the central coast region of modern Vietnam, in the **16th** and **17th centuries**. Then, in the **18th century**, it moved into territory in the Mekong Delta region that had previously been part of the Cambodian state.

For much of its independent history, power in Vietnam was in the hands of two antagonistic rival families, with the emperor occupying a figurehead position. Following a major rebellion at the end of the **18th century**, Vietnam was united under the first Nguyen emperor, Gia Long, in **1802**. He and his successors appeared successfully to have achieved the political unity Vietnam had lacked for centuries, but with the court deeply affected by conservative Confucian values, it was no match for the challenge of a technologically superior invader when the French embarked on the colonial conquest of the country. Initially establishing themselves in southern Vietnam at the beginning of the **1860s**, the French went on to gain colonial control of the whole of Vietnam in the **1880s**.

The French were determined to make Vietnam a profitable colony, but their policies to achieve this goal met with mixed success. Northern Vietnam had little to offer in terms of export commodities apart from coal and zinc mines. In the south, on the other hand, rice was grown for export in the Mekong Delta and there were also exports from the large rubber plantations established in the early years of the **20th century**.

Resentment of French rule led to periodic efforts at rebellion, which the colonial power repressed harshly. The French made much of their commitment to having a 'civilising mission' in Vietnam, and under their rule there was an expansion of modern education, but by the **1920s** there were clear indications that modern nationalists were determined to pursue the goal of full independence. In major revolts in **1930–31**, it became clear that Vietnamese who had embraced communist ideology would be major players in the nationalist struggle. By this stage, Ho Chi Minh had emerged as a key figure in the Vietnamese Communist Party.

At the end of the Second World War, with the French seriously weakened, the Vietnamese communists took the political initiative and, in September **1945**, declared independence from the French. French determination to return and reimpose colonial rule meant that negotiations to prevent a military clash were doomed to failure, and in **1946**, hostilities broke out between the French and the communist-led Viet Minh front. This, the First Indochina War, lasted until **1954** and ended in a humiliating French defeat. With the United States supporting Vietnamese anti-communists, Vietnam's territory was divided into a communist north and an anti-communist south.

Determined to gain control of the whole of Vietnam, the communist government based in Hanoi began a guerrilla warfare campaign in the south with the aim of toppling the American-backed government in Saigon (now Ho Chi Minh City). By the early **1960s**, this campaign was becoming transformed into a war involving conventional battles. In response, the United States committed its military forces to support the anti-communists and, by **1965**, the Second Indochinese War (the American War in Vietnam) was being fought.

Despite sustaining heavy casualties, the Hanoi government's determination to achieve its goals, coupled with the weakness of the government in Saigon and growing opposition to the war in the United States, led to an American decision to withdraw its troops from Vietnam. The communists finally achieved victory in **1975**, bringing the whole of Vietnam under their control.

In the decade after their victory, the communists imposed strict control over both politics and the economy. By the late **1980s**, the lack of economic success and the costs involved in the occupation of Cambodia led to the leadership rethinking its policies. Vietnam withdrew from Cambodia and state control of the economy was relaxed to a significant degree. While liberalisation of the economy continued through the **1990s**, the Communist Party's control over politics has remained as strong as ever.

Vietnam joined ASEAN in **1995**.

Vietnam has a population of 72 million.

Time chart of modern Southeast Asian history

The simplified time chart indicates the growth of external (colonial) control over Southeast Asia, starting from the beginning of the nineteenth century when, with the exception of Indonesia and the Philippines, and with the minor British settlement of Penang, the bulk of the region was still under traditional rule. Examined as a whole the time chart emphasises how relatively recent was European expansion in Southeast Asia. It also gives emphasis to the way in which the Second World War represented a sharp break with the past and played a vital part in setting the scene for the achievement of independence by the countries of Southeast Asia.

One cautionary point is necessary. The shading on the time chart represents the expansion of colonial control so that for Vietnam, for instance, the shading indicates the existence of French control over all of the country from the mid-1880s. As has been made clear in this text, there was continuing resistance to French rule after the 1880s. Moreover, it should be further recognised that the degree of impact of colonial control in, say, Malaya, was much greater as at 1939 than in 1919 even though British control extended over the whole country before this latter date. In brief, what the time chart depicts is the broad fact of colonial rule rather than the details of resistance and rebellion and the degree of impact of external rule.

A different hatching is used to indicate continuing external rule after the Second World War since in each case where such rule continued external control was either disputed by movements demanding independence (Cambodia, Indonesia, Laos, Vietnam) or the colonial power had given some form of undertaking to grant independence (Burma, Malaysia, Singapore). Even Brunei's long-delayed accession to independence took place against a background in which Britain had made clear its intention to give up its role as a protecting power.

Time chart of modern Southeast Asian history

	1800	1820	1840	1860	1880	1900	1910	1920	1930	1940	1950	1960	1980
BRUNEI	Once exercising power over much of coastal Borneo and the Sulu Archipelago, Brunei was a declining power in the early 19th century		1844 Brunei loses control of Sarawak to James Brooke		1877 Brunei cedes Sabah to the North Borneo Co. / 1888 Brunei becomes a British Protectorate		1906 Britain appoints a Resident to administer Brunei					Brunei decides not to join Malaysia in 1963	Brunei gains independence in 1984
BURMA	Burma governed by the Konbaung Dynasty since 1752	1824–26 First Burma War		1852–53 Second Burma War		1885 Third Burma War	Burma governed as a British colony until Second World War				1948 Burma gains independence		
CAMBODIA	Cambodia by the end of the 18th century a weak state paying tribute to Thailand and Vietnam			1864 Cambodia comes under French Colonial control			Cambodia governed as a French 'Protectorate' until Second World War				1953 Cambodia gains independence		
EAST TIMOR	By the end of the 18th century East Timor had been part of Portugal's colonial empire for over 200 years										1975 Indonesia invades East Timor	2002 East Timor becomes independent
INDONESIA	By the end of the 18th century Dutch control extended over Java and the principal port centres in much of the archipelago			Throughout the 19th century Dutch control slowly extended over the archipelago, advances taking place in the period 1890–1910			Indonesia (Netherlands Indies) governed as a Dutch colony until the Second World War				1949 Indonesia gains independence from the Dutch, from 1946 to 1949		
LAOS	No single Lao state existed at the end of the 18th century. A series of principalities and petty states existed as vassals of stronger neighbours				1893 France established control over almost all of the territory of modern Laos		Laos governed as a French 'Protectorate' until the Second World War				1953 Laos gains independence		
MALAYSIA	At the end of the 18th century the only parts of modern Malaysia under foreign control were Penang and Malacca	1824 control of Malacca passes from Holland to Britain	From the early 1870s onwards Britain gains colonial control of the Malay states			Modern peninsular Malaysia governed under British colonial control					1957 Malaysia gains independence as the federation of Malaysia		

Second World War and Japanese Interregnum.

	1800	1820	1840	1860	1880	1900	1910	1920	1930	1940	1950	1960	1980
PHILIPPINES	At the end of the 18th century the Philippines had experienced two centuries of slowly expanding Spanish rule					1898 Unsuccessful revolt against Spanish rule	1899 Outbreak of Spanish-American War leads to American colonial control		1935 Introduction of internal self-government		1946 Philippines gains independence		
SINGAPORE	At the end of the 18th century Singapore was an almost uninhabited island 1819 Raffles founded modern Singapore				Singapore governed as a British colony as part of the Straits Settlements in association with Penang and Malacca							1963 Singapore gains independence	
THAILAND	At the end of the 18th century Thailand was growing in power under the leadership of the new Chakri Dynasty			1851 King Mongkut ascends throne 1868 King Chulalongkorn ascends throne					1932 Revolution ends Thai King's position as an absolute ruler				
VIETNAM	Just after the end of the 18th century, Vietnam was united under the Nguyen Dynasty in 1802			1859–67 France seizes southern Vietnam to establish the colony of Chochinchina		1885–86 France seizes central and northern Vietnam (Annam and Tonkin)		Vietnam under French colonial rule			1954 Vietnam gains independence		
SOME CROSS REFERENCES	1815 Napoleon defeated at Waterloo 1832 Great Reform Bill enacted in Britain		1848 'Year of Revolution' in Europe	1867 Opening of Suez Canal 1861–65 American Civil War 1870–71 Franco-Prussian War	1880–1900 European colonial advance in Africa 1899–1902 Boer War		1917 Soviet Revolution 1911 Chinese Revolution 1914 First World War		1929–30 Beginning of Great Depression 1939 Second World War		1947 India gains independence		1991 Dissolution of the Soviet Union

Second World War and Japanese Interregnum

Maps .

CAMBODIA

INDONESIA

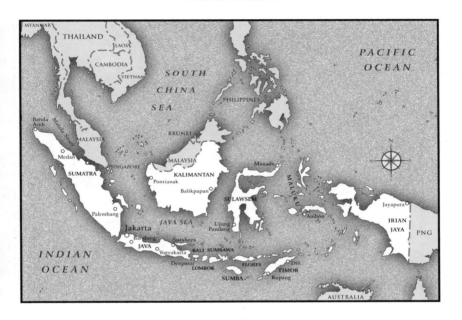

Laos

PENINSULAR MALAYSIA

EAST MALAYSIA

BRUNEI

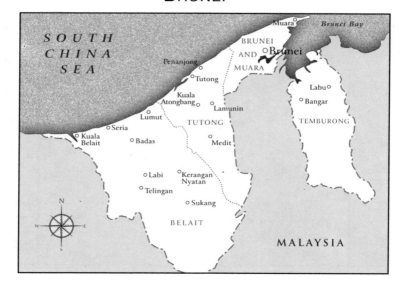

MYANMAR

INDIA

CHINA

BANGLA-
DESH

Myitkyina ○

Irrawaddy R.

Lashio ○

Salween R.

○ Mandalay

○ Ava

Pagan ○   Taunggi

Meiktila ○

Thazii ○

Pyinmana ○

Prome ○

○ Toungoo

Sandoway ○

LAOS

BAY

OF

BENGAL

Pegu ○

Yangon
(Rangoon)

Bassein ○

○ Moulmein

THAILAND

○ Tavoy

*Andaman
Islands*
(India)

N

W   E

○ Tenasserim

PHILIPPINES

SINGAPORE

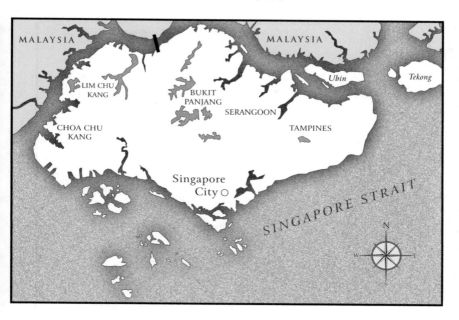

THAILAND

Vietnam

Further reading

Over the past thirty years, the number of books published on Southeast Asian subjects has increased enormously. As a result, many earlier publications have become distinctly out-of-date. The following suggested readings should be regarded as an *introduction* only to what is available. In almost every case, the books listed provide bibliographies that can be consulted for additional material. Some of the items listed are now out of print, but are generally available in libraries.

General historical and political studies of Southeast Asia

Anderson, B.R.O'G., *Imagined Communities*, London, 1983.

——, *The Spectre of Comparisons: Nationalism, Southeast Asia and the World*, London, 1998.

Hall, D.G.E, *A History of South-East Asia*, 4th edition, London, 1981.

Osborne, M., *Southeast Asia: An Introductory History*, 8th edition, Sydney, 2000.

——, *The Mekong: Turbulent Past, Uncertain Future*, New York and Sydney, 2000.

Reid, A., *Southeast Asia in the Age of Commerce, 1450–1680*, New Haven, Conneticut, 1988.

——, *Southeast Asia in the Early Modern Era: Trade, Power and Belief*, Ithaca, New York, 1993.

Steinberg, D.J. ed., *In Search of Southeast Asia: A Modern History*, revised edition, New York, 1987.

Stuart-Fox, M., *China and Southeast Asia*, Sydney, 2002.

Tarling, N. ed., *The Cambridge History of Southeast Asia*, 2 vols, Cambridge, 1992.

Tarling, N., *Southeast Asia: A Modern History*, Melbourne, 2001.

Vatikiotis, M.R.J., *Political Change in Southeast Asia: Trimming the Banyan Tree*, London, 1996.

Geography

Fisher, C.A., *South-East Asia: A Social, Economic and Political Geography*, 2nd edition, London, 1966.

Hill, R.D., *Southeast Asia: People, Land and Economy*, Sydney, 2002.

Pluvier, J., *A Historical Atlas of Southeast Asia*, Leiden, 1995.

Society and economy

Elson, R.E., *The End of the Peasantry in Southeast Asia, A Social and Economic History of Peasant Livelihood, 1800–1990s*, New York, 1997.

Evans, G. ed., *Asia's Cultural Mosaic: An Anthropological Introduction*, Singapore, 1993.

Keyes, C.F., *The Golden Peninsula: Culture and Adaptation in Mainland Southeast Asia*, New York, 1977.

Pan, L. ed., *Encyclopedia of the Overseas Chinese*, London, 1999.

Swearer, D.K., *The Buddhist World of Southeast Asia*, Albany, New York, 1995.

Arts

Brown, R., *The Ceramics of South-East Asia: Their Dating and Identification*, 2nd edition, Singapore, 1988.

Gutman, P., *Burma's Lost Kingdoms: Splendours of Arakan*, Bangkok and Sydney, 2001.

Jacques, C., *Angkor*, Cologne, 1999.

Jessup, H., *Court Arts of Indonesia*, New York, 1990.

Maxwell, R., *Textiles of Southeast Asia: Tradition, Trade and Transformation*, Melbourne and New York, 1990.

Miksic, J., *Borobudur, Golden Tales of the Buddha*, Singapore, 1995.

Pisit Charoenwongsa and Subhadradis, M.C., *Thailand*, Geneva, 1978.

Rawson, P., *The Art of Southeast Asia: Cambodia, Vietnam, Thailand, Laos, Burma, Java, Bali*, London, 1967.

Early Southeast Asian history

Coedès, G., *The Making of Southeast Asia*, Berkeley, California, 1966.

Hall, K.R., *Maritime Trade and State Development in Early Southeast Asia*, Honolulu, 1984.

Higham, C., *The Archaeology of Mainland Southeast Asia*, Cambridge, 1989.

——, *The Civilization of Angkor*, London, 2001.

Mabbet, I., and Chandler, D.P., *The Khmers*, Oxford, 1995.

Marr, D.G. and Milner, A.C., eds., *Southeast Asia in the 9th to 14th Centuries*, Singapore and Canberra, 1986.

Miksic, J. ed., *Indonesian Heritage: Ancient History*, Singapore, 1996.

Tarling, N. ed., *The Cambridge History of Southeast Asia*, Vol. 1.

Vickery, M., *Society, Economics and Politics in Pre-Angkor Cambodia*, Tokyo, 1998.

Wolters, O.W., *Early Indonesian Commerce: A Study of the Origins of Srivijaya*, Ithaca, New York, 1967.

The rise and fall of the colonial empires

Christie, C.J., *A Modern History of Southeast Asia: Decolonization, Nationalism and Separatism*, London and New York, 1996.

Keay, J., *Empire's End: A History of the Far East from High Colonialism to Hong Kong*, New York, 1997.

Osborne, M., *River Road to China: The Search for the Source of the Mekong, 1866–1873*, Singapore and Sydney, 1996, New York, 1997.

Pluvier, J.M., *Southeast Asia from Colonialism to Independence*, Kuala Lumpur, 1974.

Modern Southeast Asia by country

Brunei

Ranjit Singh, D.S., *Brunei 1834–1983; The Problems of Political Survival*, Singapore, 1984.

Saunders, G., *A History of Brunei*, Kuala Lumpur, 1994.

Turnbull, C.M., *A History of Malaysia, Singapore and Brunei*, Sydney 1989.

Burma

Aung-Thwin, M., *Pagan: The Origins of Modern Burma*, Honolulu, 1985.

Cady, J.F., *A History of Modern Burma*, Ithaca, N.Y., 1958.

Maung Maung, *Burmese Nationalist Movements, 1940–48*, Honolulu, 1990.

Silverstein, J., *Burma: The Politics of Stagnation*, Ithaca, N.Y., 1978.

Smith, M., *Burma: Insurgency and the Politics of Ethnicity*, London, 1991.

Taylor, R.H., *The State in Burma*, Honolulu, 1988.

Cambodia

Chandler, D.P., *A History of Cambodia*, 2nd edition, Boulder, Colorado, 1993.

——, *The Tragedy of Cambodian History: Politics, War and Revolution Since 1945*, New Haven, Conneticut, 1991.

——, *Brother Number One: A Political Biography of Pol Pot*, Sydney, 1993.

Kiernan, B., *How Pol Pot Came to Power*, London, 1985.

——, *The Khmer Rouge Regime: Race, Power and Genocide in Cambodia, 1975–79*, New Haven, Conneticut, 1996.

Osborne, M., *The French Presence in Cochinchina and Cambodia: Rule and Response (1859–1905)*, Ithaca, New York, 1969.

——, *Before Kampuchea: Preludes to Tragedy*, Sydney, 1979.

——, *Sihanouk: Prince of Light, Prince of Darkness*, Sydney, 1994.

Vickery, M., *Cambodia: 1975–1982*, Hemel Hempstead and Sydney, 1984.

East Timor

Dunn, J., *Timor: A People Betrayed*, Milton, Queensland, 1983.

Joliffe, J., *East Timor, Nationalism and Colonialism*, Brisbane, 1978.

Krieger, H. ed., *East Timor and the International Community: Basic Documents*, Cambridge, 1997.

Martinkus, J., *A Dirty Little War*, Sydney, 2001.

Schwarz, A., *A Nation in Waiting: Indonesia's Search for Stability*, 2nd edition, Sydney, 1999.

Taylor, J.G., *East Timor: The Price of Freedom*, London, 1999.

Indonesia

Brown, C., *A Short History of Indonesia*, Sydney, 2002.

Feith, H., *The Decline of Constitutional Democracy in Indonesia*, Ithaca, New York, 1962.

Hooker, V.M. ed., *Culture and Society in New Order Indonesia*, Oxford, 1995.

Ingleson, J., *The Road to Exile: The Indonesian Nationalist Movement 1927–1934*, Singapore, 1979.

Kahin, G.McT., *Nationalism and Revolution in Indonesia*, Ithaca, New York, 1952, reprinted 1970 and subsequent editions.

Legge, J.D., *Indonesia*, 2nd edition, Sydney, 1977.

——, *Sukarno: A Political Biography*, 2nd edition, Sydney, 1985.

MacIntyre, A., *Business and Politics in Indonesia*, Sydney, 1990.

O'Rourke, K., *Reformasi: The Struggle for Power in Post-Soeharto Indonesia*, Sydney, 2002.

Ricklefs, M.C., *A History of Modern Indonesia Since c.1300*, London, 1993.

Schwarz, A., *A Nation in Waiting: Indonesia's Search for Stability*, 2nd edition, Sydney, 1999.

Sundhaussen, U., *The Road to Power: Indonesian Military Politics, 1945–1967*, Kuala Lumpur, 1982.

Vatakiotis, M., *Indonesian Politics Under Suharto*, London, 1993.

Laos

Evans, G., *The Politics of Ritual and Remembrance: Laos since 1975*, Chiang Mai, 1998.

——, *A Short History of Laos: The Land In Between*, Sydney, 2002.

Kremmer, C., *Stalking the Elephant Kings: In Search of Laos*, Sydney, 1997.
Stuart-Fox, M., *Laos: Politics and Society*, London, 1986.
——, *A History of Laos*, Melbourne, 1997

Malaysia

Allen, C. ed., *Tales from the South China Seas*, London, 1983.
Butcher, J.G., *The British in Malaya, 1880–1941*, Kuala Lumpur, 1979.
Crouch, H., *Government and Society in Malaysia*, Sydney, 1996.
Hooker, V.M., *A Short History of Malaysia*, Sydney, forthcoming.
Kratoska, P., *The Japanese Occupation of Malaya*, Sydney, 1998.
Milne, R.S. and Mauzy, D.K., *Malaysia: Tradition, Modernity and Islam*, Boulder, Colorado, 1986.
Milner, A.C., *Kerajaan: Malay Political Culture on the Eve of Colonial Rule*, Tucson, Arizona, 1982.
——, *The Invention of Politics in Colonial Malaya: Contesting Nationalism and Expansion of the Public Sphere*, Sydney, 1998.
Pringle, R.M., *Rajahs and Rebels: The Ibans of Sarawak Under Brooke Rule, 1841–1941*, Ithaca, New York, 1970.

The Philippines

Corpuz, O.D., *The Philippines*, Englewood Cliffs, New Jersey, 1965.
Cushner, N.P., *Spain in the Philippines: From Conquest to Revolution*, Quezon City, 1970.
Friend, T., *Between Two Empires: The Ordeal of the Philippines, 1929–1946*, New Haven, Conn., 1965.
Karnow, S., *In Our Own Image*, London, 1990.
McCoy, A.W. and de Jesus, E. *Philippine Social History: Global Trade and Local Transformations*, Sydney, 1982.
May, R.J. and Nemenzo, F. *The Philippines after Marcos*, London, 1985.
Paredes, R.R., *Philippine Colonial Democracy*, New Haven, Conneticut, 1988.
Rosenberg, D.A. ed., *Marcos and Martial Law in the Philippines*, Ithaca, New York, 1979.
Steinberg, D.J., *The Philippines: A Singular and Plural Place*, Boulder, Colorado, 1982.

Singapore

Chan Heng Chee, *The Dynamics of One Party Dominance: The PAP at the Grass Roots*, Singapore, 1976.

——, *A Sensation of Independence: A Political Biography of David Marshall*, Singapore, 1984.

Chew, E.C.F., and Lee, E., *A History of Singapore*, Singapore, 1991.

George, T.J.S., *Lee Kuan Yew's Singapore*, London, 1973.

Josey, A., *Lee Kuan Yew*, revised edition, Singapore, 1971.

Lam Peng Er and Tan, K.Y.L. eds., *Lee's Lieutenants: Singapore's Old Guard*, Sydney, 1999.

Lee Kuan Yew, *The Singapore Story: Memoirs of Lee Kuan Yew*, Singapore, 1998.

——, *From Third World to First: The Singapore Story: 1965–2000*, New York, 2000.

Milne, R.S. and D.K. Mauzy, *Singapore: The Legacy of Lee Kuan Yew*, Boulder, Colorado, 1990.

Minchin, J., *No Man is an Island*, Sydney, 1986.

Turnbull, C.M., *A History of Singapore, 1819–1975*, Kuala Lumpur, 1977.

Thailand

Batson, B.J., *The End of the Absolute Monarchy in Siam*, Singapore, 1984.

Bunnag, T., *The Provincial Administration of Siam, 1829–1915*, Kuala Lumpur, 1977.

Chakrabongse, Prince Chula, *Lords of Life: The Paternal Monarchy of Bangkok, 1782–1932*, New York, 1960.

Girling, J.L.S., *Thailand: Society and Politics*, Ithaca, New York, 1981.

Hewison, K., *Politics and Power in Thailand: Essays in Political Economy*, Manila, 1989.

Keyes, C.F., *Thailand*, Boulder, Colorado, 1987.

Stowe, J.A., *Siam becomes Thailand*, London, 1991.

Vella, W., *Chaiyo!*, Honolulu, 1978.

Wright, J.J., *The Balancing Act: A History of Modern Thailand*, Bangkok, 1991.

Wyatt, D.K., *A Short History of Thailand*, New Haven, Conneticut, 1984.

Vietnam

Buttinger, J., *A Dragon Embattled: A History of Colonial and Post-Colonial Vietnam*, 2 vols, New York, 1967.

Duiker, W.J., *The Rise of Nationalism in Vietnam, 1900–1941*, Ithaca, New York, 1982.

——, *Ho Chi Minh*, New York and Sydney, 2000.

Huynh Kim Khanh, *Vietnamese Communism, 1925–1941*, Ithaca, New York, 1982.

Jamieson, N.L., *Understanding Vietnam*, Berkeley, California, 1993.

Kahin, G.McT., *Intervention: How America Became Involved in Vietnam*, New York, 1986.

Karnow, S., *Vietnam: A History*, London, 1983.

Langguth, A.J., *Our Vietnam: The War 1954–1975*, New York, 2000.

McAlister, J., and Mus, P., *The Vietnamese and their Revolution*, New York, 1970.

Marr, D. G., *Vietnamese Anti-Colonialism, 1885–1925*, Berkeley, California, 1971.

——, *Vietnamese Tradition on Trial, 1920–1945*, Berkeley, California, 1981.

——, *Vietnam 1945*, Berkeley, California, 1995.

Osborne, M., *The French Presence in Cochinchina and Cambodia: Rule and Response (1859–1905)*, Ithaca, New York, 1969.

Shaplen, R., *Bitter Victory*, New York, 1986.

Turley, W., *The Second Indochina War*, Boulder, Colorado, 1986.

Warner, D., *The Last Confucian*, New York, 1963.

——, *Not Always on Horseback: An Australian Correspondent at War and Peace in Southeast Asia, 1961–1993*, Sydney, 1997.

Woodside, A.B., *Vietnam and the Chinese Model*, Cambridge, Massachusetts, 1971.

——, *Community and Revolution in Modern Vietnam*, Boston, 1976.

Index

Note: Throughout the following index place names and religious monuments are followed by the country in which they are located in brackets.